PURITY AND AUSPICIOUSNESS
IN INDIAN SOCIETY

INTERNATIONAL STUDIES
IN
SOCIOLOGY AND SOCIAL ANTHROPOLOGY

General Editor

K. ISHWARAN

VOLUME XLIII

JOHN B. CARMAN AND FRÉDÉRIQUE A. MARGLIN (EDS.)

PURITY AND AUSPICIOUSNESS IN INDIAN SOCIETY

LEIDEN — E. J. BRILL — 1985

PURITY AND AUSPICIOUSNESS IN INDIAN SOCIETY

EDITED BY

JOHN B. CARMAN and FRÉDÉRIQUE APFFEL MARGLIN

LEIDEN — E. J. BRILL — 1985

ISBN 90 04 07789 8

PRINTED IN THE NETHERLANDS BY E. J. BRILL

CONTENTS

Introduction

FRÉDÉRIQUE APFFEL MARGLIN

Smith College, Northampton, U.S.A.

THE PRESENT VOLUME consists of the proceedings[1] of a conference which took place in May 1980 under the auspices of the Conference on Religion in South India on the topic of "Purity and Auspiciousness." In soliciting papers for this conference, John Carman and I sent to prospective participants a summary statement on research findings to date on the concepts of auspiciousness and purity. In this introduction I will enlarge this statement so as to situate the issues with which this volume is concerned.

Up until very recently, the concept of 'auspiciousness' has received far less attention than that of 'purity.' An early work giving an important place to both is Srinivas' study of the Coorgs (1952). In that work, Srinivas presents the two complexes of *maṅgala* (auspicious) on the one hand and of *polé* (impure) and *maḍi* (pure) on the other hand as separate categories. The term *maṅgala* designates rites of passage in the life-cycle, the wedding ceremony being the *maṅgala* ceremony par excellence, so much so that the word *maṅgala* has come to mean the marriage ceremony. Other *maṅgalas* are girls' puberty rituals and the celebration for a woman who has had ten surviving children.

Polé and *maḍi* are concepts which are intimately connected to the social structure (ibid.:108). In his interpretation of the ethnographic data, Srinivas creates two overarching categories. By joining *maṅgala* to *maḍi* he arrives at the notion of good-sacredness. By joining inauspiciousness to impurity, he arrives at the notion of bad-sacredness. The effect of creating these super-categories is to blur the distinction between auspiciousness and purity.

In their review of Srinivas' work on the Coorgs, Dumont and Pocock further minimize the difference between the categories of auspiciousness and purity. They write:

> ...we can ask ourselves whether the auspiciousness of marriage is really as foreign to the basic ideas of purity and impurity as an analysis in terms of solidarity would lead us to believe... It is remarkable that marriage is one of the rare "rites of passage" in which, unlike birth, girls' puberty or death, no impurity is involved; accordingly it is the most auspicious ceremony. It is possible, then, to suppose that the condition of the bride and groom in marriage is similar to that of people of a superior caste. (Dumont and Pocock, 1959:33)

Even though such a reading of Srinivas' material proved to be enormously influential in anthropological studies, it was not the only one. Influenced by Srinivas' work as well as informed by on the ground observation in South Indian villages, John Carman stressed the difference between the values of auspiciousness and those of purity. Speaking of the two opposites to the state of ritual impurity, this is what he writes in *Village Christians and Hindu Culture:*

> One is the state of ritual purity required to carry out certain religious acts....It is, however, the second 'opposite' to ritual impurity which is more significant in the lives of most village Hindus. This is the 'auspicious' state. Whereas ritual purity is considered an unusual and temporary condition, except for ascetics who have placed themselves outside the ordinary structure of society, it is the auspicious state which is the quintessence of normal life in society. It is most fully realized in the state of marriage, and most clearly symbolized in the emblems which the married woman is allowed and expected to wear. (Carman and Luke, 1968:32)

At the end of this passage Carman refers in a footnote to Srinivas' work on the Coorgs. Carman's observations and his reading of Srinivas, coming as they did from a historian of religion writing about Christianity in India, remained largely (if not totally) ignored among social scientists. The publication in 1966 of Dumont's brilliant work on the caste system, *Homo Hierarchicus* (first translated into English in 1970), contributed greatly to the dominant interpretative view which collapsed the categories of auspiciousness and purity.

Srinivas himself in his second ethnography, *The Remembered Village* (1976), seems to have abandoned auspiciousness as a major cultural category. Like the Coorg ethnography, Srinivas' later ethnographic work is situated in Karnataka. In the later work the whole *maṅgala* complex is absent; the word is not even to be found in the glossary, whereas the words *polé* and *maḍi* are recorded.

Such was the influence of Dumont's work that Carman himself apparently lost sight of the distinction between auspiciousness and purity (see Carman's paper in the present volume, p. 118).

To my knowledge, it is not until 1976, with the publication of Khare's work on food, that the issue of the distinctiveness of the two axes of auspiciousness/inauspiciousness and purity/impurity is again taken up in the literature. In Khare's discussion of foods at birth and death ceremonies, he notices that the mother and the cremator are both impure but that the food for the mother is auspicious whereas the food for the cremator is inauspicious:

> We have further noted food cycles at birth as being essentially and predominantly festive, bearing little affinity to the mourning food cycles, although both may generate ritual pollution....It may be useful now to consider them briefly against the auspicious and impure axis and see how the two fundamentally differ, despite several superficial similarities.
> (Khare 1976:184)

Reflecting on the difference between the fasts and festivals observed by the women and the 'spiritual fasts' observed by men, Khare is led to generalize about the meaning of purity and of auspiciousness. This is what he writes:

> ...the value of ritual purity that must be ultimately directed towards either maintaining or catering to religious aims of the individual appears conceptually distinguished from auspiciousness which represents a dominant Hindu value of collective life.
> (Ibid.:157)

In making such a generalization there is of course the difficulty of translation; what does the word 'purity' stand for exactly? This is a question raised by several participants in the conference and addressed in several papers in this volume. Khare himself warns social anthropologists that there are many words which are translated by the single word 'purity' (Khare 1976a:79). In the above quote, however, as in most of Khare's two books, the word 'purity' is used without a corresponding indigenous word. Here he connects purity with the religious pursuit of the individual and further specifies that unless a householder intends to become a *sannyasi*, he emphasizes auspiciousness (1976:157). This interpretation would restrict the meaning of purity to the pursuit of renunciation and liberation, which indeed has been recognized by many as being an individual's pursuit. However, another strand of purity cannot be dissociated from the whole social edifice. Dumont especially has persuasively argued that the principle of the pure and the impure underlies the caste system as a whole. This association between the whole social system and purity is by no means restricted to Dumont and is fairly widely held by many Indianists. If such a view has any merit, and I for one think it does, it is difficult to dissociate purity from the collective.

The papers by Jaini and Tambiah, included in this volume, on the Jain and Buddhist understandings of these concepts are relevant to this discussion. Jaini and Tambiah show rather conclusively that both Jains and Theravāda Buddhists reject the notion of purity *in this world.* For Jains and Buddhists, purity exists only in the sphere of the monk, the one who has left this world, society, and family, for the pursuit of enlightenment. In both the Jain and the Buddhist case, explicit contrasts are made with the Hindu tradition in which purity resides in the brahmin who is in and of this world, a householder, and not a renouncer. In the Jain case, this is made abundantly clear by classifying auspiciousness and inauspiciousness (*śubha* and *aśubha*) as subcategories of *aśuddha* (impurity). *Śubha* and *aśubha* are values of this world, things "capable of producing worldly happiness and unhappiness" (Jaini: this volume). The category of *aśuddha* is opposed to that of *śuddha* (purity) as that which is impure, meaning that which is "non-productive of activities leading to salvation" (Ibid.). In other words what Jaini describes is a situation in which purity simply does not exist in this world. Purity is only what pertains to the person who has renounced this world, or to actions in this world leading to salvation. The latter of course corresponds to Khare's statement; but it is precisely the presence of purity other than that leading to salvation and other-worldliness which differentiates Hinduism from both Jainism and Buddhism.

Thus it seems to me that the contrast set up by Khare between auspiciousness and purity does not hold. This is an issue that is explored in many of the papers in this volume: what values and actions does the auspicious/inauspicious axis stand for and what does the purity/impurity axis stand for? What are the relationship(s) between them?

Khare summarizes his findings about food cycles with a scheme of four different axes: festivity/mourning; auspiciousness/inauspiciousness; purity/impurity; highness/lowness (1976a:71). By setting up a separate category of highness/lowness, Khare once again dissociates 'purity' from hierarchy. I would, however, hold with Dumont that some form of purity is at the heart of hierarchy. As to the first two axes, based on my own research, I would argue that festivity and mourning are specific instances of the values of auspiciousness and inauspiciousness. It is true—as Inden points out in this volume—that there are many indigenous words which are translated by the term auspicious; some of these are *maṅgala*, *śubha*, *kalyāṇa*. A careful linguistic mapping of these different terms might help us discriminate more finely between different instances of what we call the 'auspicious.' Even though such a work remains to be done, I would tentatively argue that whatever the differences between various kinds of 'auspiciousness' may be, we are not warranted in making such a radical distinction between festivity and auspiciousness as to assign them to distinct axes. Thus we come back to the two axes pure/impure and auspicious/inauspicious.

In my own work, based on field research among the *devadāsī*s (literally 'female servants of the deity') of Puri (Orissa), I have also made a clear distinction between the polar opposites of auspiciousness and inauspiciousness and those of purity and impurity.[2] The *devadāsī*s are called the 'auspicious women' (*maṅgaḷa nārī*)[3] and they are the ones who sing the 'auspicious songs' (*mangaḷa gīta*). These women are, however, never allowed into the inner sanctum of the temple of Jagannātha, the latter being the locus of their ritual duties. Such a prohibition is significant since all the other ritual specialists as well as the public at large are allowed in the inner sanctum at certain times of the day. This prohibition is linked to the *devadāsī*s' status as courtesans and the impurity of sex. The tension between the auspiciousness and the impurity of the *devadāsī*s has been a major focus of my work. In my paper in this volume I attempt to characterize the nature of the auspicious/inauspicious opposition and contrast it with the pure/impure opposition.

Veena Das' work is also relevant to the concerns of this volume. Although the distinctions that she identifies in her earlier work (1977) are not phrased in terms of the categories of the auspicious and the inauspicious, they bear a striking similarity to my own discussion of these categories. In her analysis of the Gṛhya Sūtras of Gobhila she shows that the right/left opposition corresponds to a life/death opposition. She points out that the sacred is divided with reference to different kinds of oppositions. One opposition is that between right and left and the other one is that of the pure and the impure. She highlights the fact that the two sets of oppositions are not equivalent (Das 1977:119).

In the second edition of her book, Das has added an epilogue (1982) in which she rephrases her earlier analyses in terms of the auspicious/inauspicious and purity/impurity axes. Das associates auspiciousness and inauspiciousness with events, an argument made by Madan in this volume.[4] Unlike Madan, however, she identifies these terms with the opposites of life and death:

> ...auspicious events may be said to be associated with life, and are represented by the right side of the body, while inauspicious events may be said to be associated with death, and are represented by the left side of the body...
>
> ...the categories of auspicious and inauspicious [...] seem to me to refer respectively to events involving life and future, and events involving death and the termination of a future...
>
> (Veena Das 1982:143-144)

The following diagram taken from Veena Das' new epilogue, summarizes her findings: (Das 1982:143)

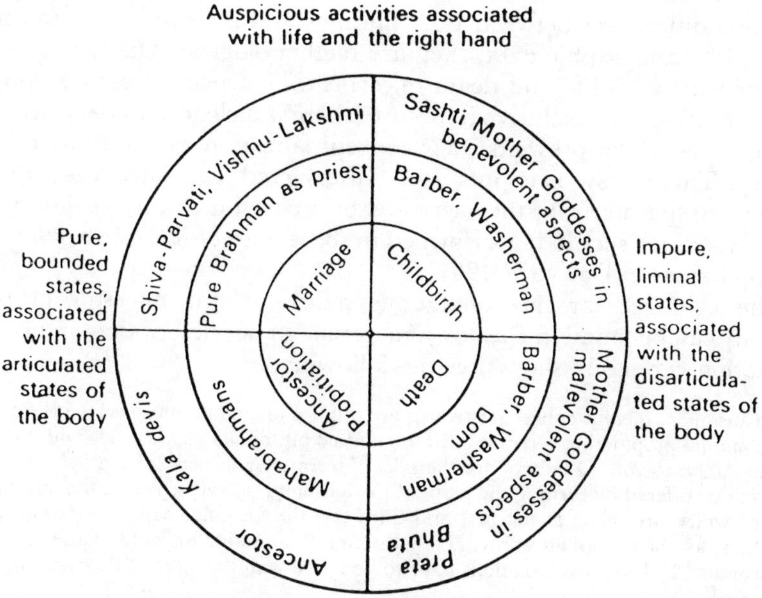

Even though she does not title the bottom end of her vertical axis, the rest of the diagram leads us to expect that it represents "inauspicious activities associated with death and the left hand." Childbirth is placed in the auspicious/impure quadrant, death in the inauspicious/impure one and ancestor worship in the inauspicious/pure one. These classifications differ both from Madan's and my own findings. In this volume Madan argues that it is not birth or death by themselves which are auspicious or inauspicious but their occurrence under a conjunction of other events, especially planetary ones. In particular, he points out that the birth of a son, which is normally an auspicious event, can sometimes be very inauspicious due to certain astrological configurations.

In her paper for this volume, Vasudha Narayanan also points out that death is not always an inauspicious event. If death occurs to a woman whose children, especially sons, and whose husband, are alive, it is considered auspicious. If it occurs to a man of advanced age whose wife has predeceased him and whose children are alive, it is also not considered inauspicious. Thus death does not always—and perhaps only in the case of the death of the last male in a patrilineal line of descent—signify the termination of a future. Similarly a new life may threaten the future.

In my paper in this volume, I have stressed the fact that the category of ancestor and the ceremony of ancestor worship are both instances where auspiciousness and inauspiciousness are simultaneously present. I have argued that the *daitās* correspond to the category of ancestors; they are the ones who attend simultaneously to the illness and rejuvenation of the deities, as well as to their 'birth' and 'death.'

These differences between Das' findings and my own are more than differences in ethnographic data; they are methodological. Das conceives of the opposition between life and death in terms of a structural binary opposition. Such oppositions are exclusive in nature: there is a clear boundary between the two opposites which prevents their conceptualization as being fused into one category. This is how Das puts it: "...the sacred associated with life is kept completely separate from the sacred associated with death, as the injunction that no weddings should be performed in the month of *shraddha* when ancestors are propitiated." (Das 1977:120)

The evidence for the ambiguous nature of the ancestor propitiation ceremony can be found in Das' own material. In her description of the ancestor propitiation ceremony she writes the following:

> For instance, there are three pits which are dug for ancestors in a special enclosure during the annual propitiating ceremony. In the middle pit, oblations are made with the formula, "adoration to you, O fathers, for the sake of terror, for the sake of sap" and this oblation has to be offered by turning the palm of the left hand upwards. But in the other two oblations which are made at the first and third pit, the formulae say "Adoration to you, O fathers, for the sake of life and vital breath" and "Adoration to you, O fathers, for the sake of comfort." These two oblations have to be made with the palm of the right hand turned upwards.
>
> (Ibid.:97)

It is clear that ancestors are propitiated for both life and death since both the right and the left hands are used. More interestingly, however, when the ancestors are invoked for the sake of "terror and sap" with the left hand the two opposites are mingled. Das seems to ignore this, and interprets the passage as an association between the left and appeasement of beings who can cause terror and discomfort and the right with the good and benevolent. The left-handed oblation, however, is not only for terror but also for sap. Sap is the vital fluid of plants and by metaphorical extension the vital fluid of humans also. In one gesture and utterance we have here the mingling of life-promoting forces and death-inspired forces. There can be no categorical separation between life and death; the two opposites can at times be found fused together. Furthermore, as Madan's and Narayanan's data show, the two opposites of life and death are not always associated with a positive and a negative pole respectively.

The categories of the auspicious and the inauspicious have also been associated with sovereignty (Marglin 1981 and Inden in this volume). As Carman shows in his second diagram in this volume (see p. 114), temporal auspiciousness is primarily embodied in the sovereign and in married women. The latter include the *devadāsīs* who represent the married state *par excellence* since they can never be widowed, being married to the deity. Carman's model makes use of Dumont's concepts of the encompassed and the encompassing.

The realm of temporal auspiciousness constitutes the innermost square of his diagram which is 'encompassed' by the realm of temporal purity, itself, 'encompassed' by various paths to trans-temporality. The relationship between the innermost and the middle square in Carman's diagram is reminiscent of Dumont's characterization of the sphere of the sovereign—and its contemporary heirs, namely the land-controlling castes—as being encompassed by the realm in which the principle of the pure and the impure reigns, namely hierarchy.

It would not be inappropriate here to discuss the concerns of this volume, specifically as they are summarized in Carman's diagram, in relation to Dumont's influential concepts of the encompassed and the encompassing.

The recognition that the principle of the pure and the impure does not account for everything in Hindu society has lead Dumont to his model of the encompassed and the encompassing. According to him, there are factors operative empirically which cannot be fitted into the ideology of the pure and the impure. These empirically observed factors are principally territoriality and the politico-economic realm. The ideology of the pure and the impure does not take into account these factors but encompasses them. Dumont identifies the realm of the encompassed—namely territory and power—with the royal domain. In contemporary India, this factor is represented mostly in the phenomenon of the dominant caste which has power by virtue of possessing the land. Thus power—the domain of the dominant castes that are heir to the older royal dominion over the land—lies outside of the principle of the pure and the impure.

In a discussion of the place of ideology Dumont (1970:36-39) identifies the factors of power and territoriality as belonging to a residual category, namely whatever the ideology does not account for. Dumont relates the power-cum-territoriality factor to ideology by identifying it as being encompassed by the latter. This encompassed status implies more than just being outside of the realm of ideology; it implies being subordinated to it. Dumont—inspiring himself from the theory of *varṇa* in the *dharmaśāstras*—sees an absolute differentiation and hierarchization between brahmin and kshatriya. The king has lost his religious prerogatives since he cannot sacrifice and requires a brahmin to perform sacrifices for him.

This distinction between status, that is purity and pollution, and power which Dumont identifies in the ancient literature, is found again in the empirically observed phenomenon of the dominant caste. The dominant caste, heir to the royal function, is an empirically observed phenomenon which cannot be fitted into the ideology of hierarchy but is subordinated to it, in other words, encompassed. This characterization indicates that the realm of power is subordinated to, as well as separate from, the realm of hierarchy. So far such a model does not conflict with the one proposed by Carman. To the correlations between the encompassed and the empirical on the one hand, and the encompassing and the ideological on the other hand, Dumont adds the distinction between the sacred and the profane. The sacred corresponds to the encompassing/ideological and the profane to the encompassed/empirical. In this identification of the encompassed and the encompassing with the profane and the sacred Dumont's views part company with those of Carman.

According to Dumont, power in India was secularized at a very early date (Dumont 1970b). Dumont thus arrives at a view of the society of caste as being divided between a religious realm in which the principle of the pure and the impure is central and a profane realm subordinated to the religious realm in which power and territory are central.

Dumont's view of the secularization of the royal function has been the focus of much criticism (Derrett 1976; Inden 1978; Marglin 1985). The problem with Dumont's model of the encompassed and the encompassing, however, is not so much one of substance as one of methodology. It is difficult to understand why in one realm—the sacred—action is not separate from ideology and meaning but in another—the profane—it is (Tambiah 1972). Such a view rests on a theoretical position which treats social reality as being divided in two. One level is considered primary and consists of 'social forms' and the other level is considered to be secondary and consists of 'representations' (Dumont 1979). In such a view, social forms are considered to be prior to other forms, the 'representations' which are 'cultural' and include such phenomena as rituals and myths. The latter are derivative of the former. The Hindu world, however, presents us with a unified reality, what Tambiah (1979) has called a 'cosmology.'

By not relegating the realm of temporal auspiciousness to the profane, as well as by including a trans-temporal realm, Carman's model differs significantly from Dumont's formulation. It does not divide the Hindu world between profane and sacred realms. It does, however, retain from Dumont's formulation the hierarchical relationship between the domain of the caste structure and that of sovereignty and married women. I would like to suggest that such a hierarchical relationship between these two domains captures but one possible mode of relating them. The encompassed status of the royal and wifely domains expresses the well-known cultural facts which place the ruler below the brahmin and the wife below her husband. I would like to propose that in certain other contexts and for different purposes the relationship can be reversed. The King is also the embodiment of a deity and as such superior to the brahmin (Bṛhadaraṇyaka Upaniṣad I.4,11 in Malamoud 1981:50) and the wife is the embodiment of the goddess Lakṣmī and as such worthy of worship by her husband (Manu IX. 26, 28). Perhaps we could adopt Malamoud's characterization of these relationships as exemplifying a "revolving hierarchy" (Malamoud 1981).

At all events, the essays in this volume all attest to the fruitfulness and the promise of considering the auspicious/inauspicious axis as representing a set of values distinct from those of the pure/impure axis. Individual contributors may differ on how these axes interrelate but they all seem to agree on their distinctness.

NOTES

1 Three participants in the conference could not contribute papers for this volume; they are McKim Marriott, Fritz Stahl, and Joanne Waghorne.

2 Not having had the advantage of having read Khare and having forgotten or misunderstood Srinivas' work on the Coorgs, such a distinction came to me the hard way, after a second period of fieldwork and much struggling with my field data.

Field research was carried out in 1975-76, summer of 1977, winter 1978-79 and summer of 1981. See Marglin 1978a, 1978b, 1978c, 1980, 1981, 1982.

3 The Oriya alphabet has two l's, one being a retroflex (ḷ). Sanskrit has no retroflex l; this accounts for the difference in transliteration of the word *maṅgaḷa*.

4 Das refers to an earlier version of Madan's paper for this volume as well as to my paper "Kings and Wives: The Separation of Status and Royal Power" (1981).

WORKS CITED

CARMAN, John and LUKE, P. Y.
1968 *Village Christians and Hindu Culture.* Great Britain:Lutterworth Press.

DAS, Veena
1977 *Structure and Cognition: Aspects of Hindu Caste and Ritual.* Delhi: Oxford University Press.
1982 "Epilogue" in *Structure and Cognition.* 2d. ed. Delhi: Oxford University Press.

DERRETT, Duncan
1976 "Rājadharma." *Journal of Asian Studies* 35, no. 4.

DUMONT, Louis
1970 *Homo Hierarchicus.* Chicago: University of Chicago Press.
1970b "The conception of kingship in ancient India" in *Religion, Politics and History in India* by Louis Dumont. Mouton.
1979 "Preface" to the new French Tel edition of *Homo Hierarchicus.*

DUMONT, Louis and POCOCK, David
1959 "Pure and Impure." In *Contributions to Indian Sociology*, No. III.

INDEN, Ronald
1978 "Ritual, Authority, and Cyclic Time in Hindu Kingship" in *Kingship and Authority in South Asia*, edited by J. F. Richards. South Asian Studies, Publication no. 3. Madison: University of Wisconsin-Madison Publication Series.

KHARE, R. S.
1976 *The Hindu Hearth and Home.* New Delhi: Vikas.
1976a *Culture and Reality.* Simla: Indian Institute of Advanced Study.

MALAMOUD, Charles
1981 "On rhetoric and semantics of puruṣārtha." In *Contributions to Indian Sociology*, n.s. vol. 15, nos. 1 & 2.

MARGLIN, Frédérique Apffel
1978a "Auspiciousness and the Devadāsīs." Paper delivered at the Conference on Religion in South India, Chambersburg, PA.
1978b "Concepts of power in Hindu thought and action." Paper presented at the Anthropological Association Meetings, Los Angeles.
1978c "The ambiguity of the fertile womb." Paper presented at the Xth International Congress of Ethnological and Anthropological Sciences, New Delhi.
1980 "Wives of the God-King: the rituals of Hindu temple courtesans." Ph. D. dissertation, Brandeis University.
1981 "Kings and Wives: the separation of status and royal power." In *Contributions to Indian Sociology*, n.s. vol. 15, nos. 1 & 2.
1982 "Types of Sexual Unions and their Implicit Meanings," in *The Divine Consort: Rādhā and the Goddesses of India*, edited by J. Hawley and D. Wulff. Berkeley, CA: Berkeley Religious Studies Series.

1985 *Wives of the God-King: the Rituals of the Devadāsīs of Puri.* Delhi, New York, Oxford: Oxford University Press.

SRINIVAS, M. N.

1952 *Religion and Society among the Coorgs of South India.* Oxford: The Clarendon Press.

1976 *The Remembered Village.* Berkeley, Los Angeles, London: University of California Press.

TAMBIAH, Stanley

1972 "Review of *Homo Hierarchicus.*" *American Anthropologist* 74, no. 4.

1979 "A Performative Approach to Ritual." The Radcliffe-Brown Lecture; *Proceedings of the British Academy*, vol. LXV. London: Oxford University Press.

Concerning the Categories *Śubha* and *Śuddha* in Hindu Culture
An Exploratory Essay

T. N. MADAN

Institute of Economic Growth, Delhi, India

I

Introductory

DURING THE LAST THREE DECADES or so the sociology of South Asian societies has been characterised by a deepening concern with the people's categories of thought over and above the attention that has long been given to the study of social organisation. This is a welcome development inasmuch as people everywhere not only engage in social behaviour but also have *ideas* about the motivations and justifications of their actions. In other words, what they do is meaningful to themselves and it is only proper that the sociologist should concern himself equally with rule-governed behaviour *and* with its significance to the actors. The work of many scholars, including Louis Dumont and M. N. Srinivas, has contributed significantly to the examination of certain ideas underlying characteristic forms of behaviour in Hindu society, notably the ideas of 'purity' and 'pollution'. There are other cognitive structures which await exploration in the context of the interrelatedness of ideology and actual behaviour. In recent years the notion of 'auspiciousness' in the senses of benediction and well-being, enveloping (as it were) the everyday life of ordinary people at the one end and of extraordinary personages such as the king at the other, has emerged as one such concern of central importance in the study of Hindu, Buddhist and Jaina cultures. In fact, in traditional thought one of the auspicious events in the life of common people was the sight of the king.

In this essay I am concerned with an attempt to clarify the notion of 'auspiciousness' and to examine its relation to 'purity' by exploring some of their meanings in Hindu or, more precisely, Brahmanical culture.[1] The published ethnographic studies on 'auspiciousness' are by no means as rich as those on 'purity' and they are certainly lacking in clarity even more than those on the latter subject. The present exercise is, therefore (to borrow T. S. Eliot's felicitous words), 'a raid on the inarticulate' and that too 'with shabby equipment'. I make the attempt, nevertheless; while doing so I use deliberately but only as far as seems reasonable the Sanskrit words *śubha* and *śuddha* instead of 'auspiciousness' and 'purity'. The former two words or derivatives from the same are in use in most languages of India. My hesitation in using the two English words throughout the essay arises from the fact that they have become omnibus words and conceal more than they reveal and this might vitiate my attempt to clarify the significance of the Hindu concepts under consideration.[2] Moreover, and more importantly, my approach to the problem makes it imperative that words actually employed in everyday speech be examined in the context of their use. Without entering into philosophical controversies or invoking the technical literature on semantics, I would like to maintain that we can learn a great deal about the meaning or meanings of a family of words by examining them in the contexts of other meanings (which is what 'use' really is). It seems to me permissible to do so for my limited purpose without going into the question of whether abstract meanings exist or not.

II

On the categories of 'śubha' and 'śuddha': notes on everyday usage

The everyday (ordinary language) use of the word *śubha* refers, it seems, most frequently and directly to time and to temporal events in relation to particular categories of people.[3] Thus the word *śubha*—or its opposite *aśubha*—is prefixed to nouns such as *samaya* or *kāla* (time) for the performance of a particular significant act. A time which may be considered auspicious for one kind of actions may not be so for another: while the night is auspicious for the worship of Mahākālī, it is not so for the worship of Viṣṇu. Similarly, *śubha* is used along with such words as *avasara* (occasion), *utsava* (festival), *ṛtu* (season), *māsa* (month), *divasa* (day), *ghaḍhi* and *kṣaṇa* (a moment or measure of time). More specifically, *śubha* qualifies *muhūrta* (astrologically appropriate moment for doing something significant) and *lagna* (the moment of sun's entry into a zodiacal space or sign). Contextually, people speak of *ārambha* (beginning), *anta* (ending), *samapanna* (completion), *āgamana* (coming), *gamana* (going), *yātrā* (pilgrimage), etc. as *śubha*, invoking benediction by doing so. *Śubha* is also employed to refer to happy events (for example, *janma*, birth, or *vivāha*, marriage) and information about them (*sūcanā*, *samācārā*), to signs (*saṅketa*), omens (*śakuna*), etc. *Śubhakārya* and *śubhācāra* respectively refer to any specific act or conduct generally which is conducive to well-being. To ensure such well-being through success and happy consequences in any kind of work, ranging from the routine to the extraordinary, people consult astrologers, priests or almanacs to find out the auspicious moment or time for—to give a few examples—wearing a new garment, buying provisions, starting on a journey, or performing a ritual. Negatively, when unfortunate events which it is feared might occur do not occur or, having occurred, do not result in misfortune, auspiciousness is said to have prevailed. The agency which ensures this well-being may be divine grace, the configuration of circumstances and/or human effort.

In all the foregoing uses of the prefix *śubha*, the focus is on the directional flow of time—on temporal sequences and critical points in them—rather than on time as such. The passage of time becomes significant through the conjunction or intersection of the trajectories of human lives and/or of such trajectories and the course of cosmic forces.

The evidence of everyday speech indicates that the notion of auspiciousness is also associated with places, objects and persons connected with the kind of events or actions mentioned above. An altar set up or a place marked out for a ritual performance is called *śubha-sthalī/sthāna.* Once the ceremony is over the altar may be demolished and the sacred area earlier set apart reverts to its daily routine uses. The kitchen (*caukā*) and the room reserved for daily worship (*pūjā-kakṣa*) are particularly auspicious places in a house so long as it is inhabited. A celestial *śubha* space which is much talked about is the *nakṣatra* (a constellation through which the moon passes at a particular time: a lunar mansion). Certain directions (*diśā*) and cardinal points in space are also regarded as *śubha* or *aśubha.* Thus facing the east while performing a ritual is regarded as desirable through its association with sunrise and facing the south is regarded as undesirable through its association with death.

A *tīrthasthāna*, or place of pilgrimage, located on the bank of a river or a body of water, is regarded as holy and a pilgrimage (*yātrā*) to it is auspicious. The holiness of the place and the auspiciousness of the visit are greatly enhanced if two or more rivers merge there: it is then elevated to the status of *saṅgama*, that is the place from where two or more streams flow together.[4] India's most holy place of pilgrimage—the *tīrtharāja*, or the king of places of pilgrimages—is Prayāg (in Uttar Pradesh) where the holy rivers Gaṅgā and Yamunā and the subterranean Sarasvatī meet and where the famous twelve-yearly bathing festival of *kumbha* is held whenever a particular astrological conjunction (*yoga*) occurs. The focus is on movement, which is what *yātrā* denotes and on 'crossing over' or 'reaching forward' from a less to a more desirable state of being, achieved by a ritual bathing in the holy waters, which is what *tīrtha* signifies: in the words of a Kashmiri Brahman informant, 'more than the impurities of the outer body (*tana*) it is the impurities of the mind (*mana*) that are thus washed away'. As in the case of time, it is not a place as such but what can possibly happen there to certain categories of people that marks it out as auspicious: we are once again confronted with the notion of intersection of the trajectories of cosmic forces, symbolised by moving planets and flowing rivers, and human lives.

Besides points in time and space, certain objects also are considered auspicious. The most notable example is the *kalaṣa*, a metal (gold, silver, copper or brass) or earthen vessel containing water from a river (or rivers) and other auspicious substances such as dry fruits.[5] The Kashmiri Brahmans treat it as a representation of Ganeśa, the deity who removes obstacles (*vighnahartā*) and bestows success on the works of human beings (*siddhidātā*) and thus symbolises auspiciousness. The *kalaṣa* is associated with the *commencement* of a ritual, when it is consecrated and worshipped, and with its *completion* when its contents are distributed by sprinkling the worshippers with the water and, to cite the practice of Kashmiri Brahmans again, offering them the walnuts, earlier placed in the vessel, to eat: doing so is considered to be conducive to well-being.

The adjective *śubha* is applied in everyday speech to actors (*kartā*) when they are seen performing actions which are conducive to joy and well-being (*śubhakārya*) or when they symbolise these states. For instance, and crucially, a *śubhacintaka* (well-wisher) is one who entertains good thoughts about another's influence on the course of the latter's life. One who conveys good news is called *śubhasūcanī.* A specific usage among the upper castes in the Hindi-speech areas worth mentioning here is the reference to prostitutes as *maṅgalamukhī*, that is one seeing whose face produces well-being. The distinction between the state of auspiciousness and the creative agent (*maṅgalakāraka* or *kalyāṇakāraka*) is most important as is the relation between the two (the signification). The point to note about these usages and similar others is that it is not the person himself or herself who is auspicious but rather his or her intentions, actions, or even merely the presence (and witnessing the same), which are so and are, therefore, expected to have happy consequences. The ultimate source of auspiciousness is, of course, the divinity (cf. Carman 1974: 172, 255).

A crucial contribution to the explication of the significance of the category *śubha* comes from the speech of priests and astrologers which is an element in the conversation of those who consult these specialists. Such people believe that their lives are subject to the influence of the nine *graha* headed by *sūrya* (sun) and including *bṛhaspati*, *budha*, *candramā*, *ketu*, *maṅgala*, *rāhu*, *śaniṣcara* and *śukra* (corresponding to moon, jupiter, mercury, dragon's tail, mars, dragon's head, saturn and venus). These *graha* are classified into two categories, namely *śubha* (beneficent) and *aśubha* or *krūra* (cruel, fierce, formidable, maleficent). Only three of these—*bṛhaspati*, *candramā*, *śukra*—were described to me by my Kashmiri Brahman informants as being *śubha*; *budha* is considered as 'impotent' or neutral and the rest as fierce. It does not, however, really matter very much to a human being what the nature of a *graha* is except insofar as any one of them, or any combination of them (*yoga*), comes to have a dominant influence on the course of his life trajectory as a result of the aspect of these heavenly beings. This fact of astral influence is called *daśā*, that is the condition and fate of a human being as affected by the movement of a *graha*. These planetary movements affect the lives of people variously depending primarily upon the time (*kāla*) and place (*sthāna*) of their birth. Thus even a maleficent *graha* may bring joy, health and prosperity to an individual owing to its location in a particular place (*gṛha*) in his birth-time horoscope (*janmakuṇḍalī*) and/or the horoscope for the year (*varṣakuṇḍalī*) and the relation of this location to the *graha's* own position during a particular period of time: zodiacal spaces are classified in respect of each *graha* as his own, his friends' or his enemies' 'homes'. In this regard, the critical datum of every individual horoscope is the *lagna*, that is the zodiacal sign under which one is born: starting from there, the life trajectory of the individual can be charted which is what the casting or writing of a horoscope involves. The auspiciousness or inauspiciousness of a life trajectory is stated in degrees rather than in absolute terms. An individual is thus conceptualised as a *pātra* ('vessel') to be filled.

Now, childbirth, particularly the birth of a son, is normally an auspicious event, but it may not be so always. The configuration of *graha* and *nakṣatra* at the time of his birth may make a particular son a menace to the well-being of his parents and, therefore, his birth is considered to be an inauspicious event. In other words, the influence of his life trajectory on those of his parents may turn out to be maleficent, reinforcing the unfortunate elements of their own trajectories and weakening the beneficent ones. For example, a boy born on the *mūla nakṣatra* to a Kashmiri Brahman family is adjudged to be a potential parricide, not of course by a wilful act of murder but by virtue of the subtle influence of the one life trajectory on the other. Nobody else would accept such a child in adoption. To avert the mortal threat, he is abandoned near the entrance to a temple, or some such holy place, thus entrusting him to the care of gods. In fact, this act may be seen as one of symbolic destruction. The family priest picks up the child—the whole act is of course prearranged—and exchanges him for money and grain with the child's own family with a member of which he has a 'chance' encounter.

Such happenings are not common but Hindus generally perform rituals regularly in the effort to ward off or at least minimise the dangers posed by inauspicious births or unfavourable *daśā*. These rituals are called *upāya* or 'corrective' actions. The most notable of these rituals that has come to my notice is *tulābhāra* when the body of the endangered person is symbolically replaced by weighing him against grain, pulses and other prescribed substances which are then given away to the family priest.[6] The body is reconstituted by means of a ritual bath and, expectedly, the whole series of rites is regarded as highly dangerous to their subject.

The extent to which such rituals succeed in warding off evil is not wholly predictable for neither can auspiciousness be totally engineered nor inauspiciousness wholly averted, no matter what promotive or corrective steps may be taken. It was pointed out to me by one of my Caturvedi Brahman informants that, though the marriage of Rāma was performed at an auspicious time and the appointed time for his consecration as the king was similarly calculated, his married life was interrupted (because of the abduction of Sītā by Rāvaṇa) and finally ended in sorrow (when Sītā immolated herself); similarly his becoming the king got postponed by the fourteen years which he had to spend in exile.

Birth is normally a *śubha* event and death is *aśubha*. Yet the degree and nature of inauspiciousness of death also are determined by the time and place at which it occurs and by other related circumstances. There is a recurrent inauspicious period in every month of the lunar calendar called *pancaka*, when five *nakṣatra* are in conjunction, for the duration of which the performance of many actions is forbidden as far as possible. The cremation of a dead body during *pancaka* is considered very unfortunate but cannot be avoided. It was explained to me that the occurrence of death during such a period is replete with dangers for the journey of the dead or departed person (*preta*) into *pitṛloka* (the abode of *manes*) and is also inauspicious for the survivors five of whom may die in the ensuing year.

Death is inauspicious but widowhood is an even more unfortunate event for an upper caste Hindu woman. It brings about a drastic change in her social identity and ritual status (see, e.g., Madan 1975). Among the Kashmiri Brahmans when an old woman dies and her husband, older than her, accompanies the funeral party to cremation ground, many women loudly express the wish that they too may die the same way, survived by husband and sons.

Let me now turn to a more complex set of usages which may not appear to be covered by the foregoing analysis. The example that comes most readily to mind is the widespread practice among Hindi-speaking people of using the expression *śubhanāma* (rendered as 'good name' in Indian English) when inquiring about one another's names.[7] Similarly, a person's body or parts of it (e.g., face or palms of the hands) may be said to bear *śubhalakṣana* (auspicious signs or marks). While it would be appropriate to point out that the word *śubha* here refers to loveliness, grace, splendour, lustrousness, etc. (see, e.g., Monier-Williams 1976), it must also be noted that these qualities are not so much values as they are signs, indicative of the future course of events in an individual's life and his influence on the lives of others.[8] Kashmiri Brahmans extoll Śiva as the most benign and beneficient divinity for (to quote from a popular hymn) 'he is the one with all the *śubhalakṣana*'.

To highlight the proper usage of the word *śubha*, it may be pointed out finally that there are certain human actions which create well-being through the very fact of being performed so that one does not have to await an auspicious time for their performance. The Kashmiri Brahmans who never undertake a journey away from home except at an auspicious hour do not consider it equally necessary similarly to time the return home, which is always auspicious. Likewise, whatever is done daily, including *pūjā*, and the cooking of food, do not have to await an auspicious hour though they have to be done outside a particularly inauspicious time such as the duration of an eclipse or the presence of a dead body in the house. Some informants from Uttar Pradesh pointed to a further distinction in this regard, namely that between *vyavahārika* (conventional) and *ādhyātmika* or *paramārthika* (spiritual) actions: when an action is motivated spiritually and not undertaken merely as a matter of convention or routine, the constraint of an inauspicious period of time—such as eclipses, *malamāsa* or *devaśayana*—becomes inoperative.[9]

The foregoing selection from a thesaurus of usages (collected by me in Kashmir and Uttar Pradesh) points to the conclusion that the 'family resemblance' which obtains among them has its roots in the significance of the *passage of time* for human beings, which varies from one category of persons to another and even from one individual to another. What is crucial is not an abstract conception of time *per se*—which is neutral in character—but the intersection of cosmic and individual life trajectories which this flux entails.

Auspiciousness, then, is an absolute value which manifests as a quality of events in the lives of human actors (*pātra*) and involves the dimensions of time (*kāla*) and space (*sthāna*).

The word *śuddha*, in contrast to *śubha*, is not generally used in everyday speech to refer to events.[10] The connotation of this word is conveyed by invoking images of fullness or completeness in the specific sense of perfection. It thus refers to the most desired condition of the human body or, more comprehensively, the most desired state of being. *Śuddha* and its opposite *aśuddha* are attributes of animate beings, inanimate objects and places with which a human being comes into contact in the course of everyday life. For example, a prepubescent unmarried girl (*kanyā*), water from a holy river, unboiled milk, ghee and a temple are *śuddha*. On the other hand, contact with certain kinds of human beings (low caste Hindus or non-Hindus), animals (dogs), objects (goods made of leather), foods (beef or food cooked in impure utensils), substances (discharges from a human body), places (cremation ground), etc. causes Brahmans and other upper caste Hindus to become polluted. The notion of perfection in the sense of freedom from error or fault is extended to certain actions also as is exemplified by such expressions as *śuddhavicāra* (pure thoughts), *śuddhauccāraṇa* (correct pronunciation which is highly valued in the recitation of sacred texts), and *śuddhasvara* (normal or natural notes in music). Human thoughts, words and musical notes are thus treated (evaluated) as objects are.

Moreover, it is important to note that degrees of *śuddha*-ness are recognised as that gold is considered more *śuddha* than, say, copper, so that objects made of gold are ever pure—'purified by the movement of air', say the Kashmiri Brahmans—while objects made of other metals require to be purified by washing with water or scrubbing with clay or cowdung and water. Even more significant is the notion that, while certain objects are *śuddha*, others—notably *darbha* grass (*poa cynosuroides*), gold, food cooked on one's own hearth kept alive by fire originally lit at the time of one's marriage ritual—are not only pure in themselves but render pure whatever/whosoever comes in contact with them unless it/he is essentially impure (such as human excrement/a Śūdra). A Kashmiri Brahman begins every ritual performance by first putting on the middle finger of his right hand a 'ring' made by twisting together seven blades of *darbha* grass.[11] This 'ring' is called *pavitra*, that is something which is itself pure and also purifies the wearer. The most *pavitra* (*parmapavitra*) object for the Brahman in his *yagñopavīta*, the three-stranded cotton neck-cord that he wears from the time of his ritual initiation (*upanayana*) onwards and which symbolises and protects his ritual status as a 'twice-born' (*dvija*) Hindu. At the time of the investiture of the neophyte with the neck-cord, the Gāyatrī *mantra*[12] is whispered into his ear by the family priest and he is thus made *śuddha*, that is the perfect actor for the performance of rituals and the discharge of adulthood roles of the householder. Ethnography on the subject of purity and pollution is so detailed, though not always illuminating (see Dumont 1970), that there is little that I can hope to contribute to the discussion beyond what I have written above.

I would, however, like to suggest a relationship between the categories of *śubha* and *śuddha* in relation to the *pātra* or actor.

I take up again the event of childbirth. It is auspicious if it occurs under the right circumstances defined by the qualities of time, space and the actors concerned, particularly the child and the mother. In actuality, the rightness of circumstances is a matter of degree for it rarely happens that every factor is without blemish to make the event perfectly auspicious. But even in the best of circumstances, the event renders the child's mother and agnatic kin ritually impure and causes pollution (*aśauca*, a specific expression of *aśuddha*) to them. The child itself is also impure. This pollution, however, pales into insignificance in the light of the joy of the auspicious character of childbirth, particularly the birth of a son, which is duly celebrated through ritual performances and social ceremonies during the following eleven days, culminating in the ritual of purification. In consonance with such an evaluation of the *śubha* but *aśuddha* aspects of childbirth is the fact that it is not the pollution that death causes which is the matter of deeper concern but the inauspiciousness of the event. My Kashmiri Brahman informants are absolutely unambiguous in their statement of this fact. The pollution wears off (through the passage of time) and is removed (through the performance of rituals) step by step. It is, however, only the occurence of an auspicious event, most notably the birth of a male child, that finally removes the pall of inauspiciousness which hangs like a dark cloud on a family in which a death has occurred (see Khare 1976a: 185).

Two other types of situation may now be briefly mentioned. First, the situation where both auspiciousness and purity are considered characteristic of an event. Brahmans regard ritual initiation and marriage (the former perhaps more than the latter) as the most notable examples. Second, the situation where inauspiciousness and purity may be found to coexist: but no such situation is acknowledged in practice, emphasising the overriding quality of auspiciousness.

Speaking specifically about the Kashmiri Brahmans, their attitude to pollution is a pragmatic one. One can avoid contact with many polluting things by the exercise of care or self-restraint. Prescribed procedures, fairly often quite simple (such as washing), are available to remove the consequences of contamination resulting from contact with such things. To be cleansed of pollution when the same is unavoidable, one has not only to wash but to do so *immediately*, for example, after evacuation or *after the lapse of a period of time*, as following a birth or death in the family. Mere washing away may not meet the requirement of restoration of ritual status and certain rituals may have to be performed. Moreover, one is pure or impure in relation to someone else or an object or the performance of a particular act in a certain degree. A menstruating woman is severely polluted for the purpose of participation in rituals (particularly the feeding of *manes*) but she is not secluded nor required to eat or sleep outside the home.

The daily life of the Kashmiri Brahmans is beset by *śaṅkā* or perplexity: uncertainties as to whether to do something or not, how to do it, when to do it, and so on. The burden of such uncertainty is heavier in the context of the inauspiciousness of certain events than in the context of the impure nature of some things, for the former are not as easily manageable as the latter are.[13] A person must watch out, when he sets out from the home on an important errand, lest somebody symbolising obstruction or failure and, therefore, inauspiciousness should be encountered or—if the encounter does take place—allowed to pass by one's right side coming from the opposite direction. Among the most dreaded of such encounters is that with a priest, including one's own family priest, without whose presence no ritual performance, including the auspicious ones, is possible.[14]

Similarly, in Uttar Pradesh, an encounter with a Mahābrahman (who assists at cremation and receives gifts made by mourners after a death) is normally considered very inauspicious. However, if he is encountered by a party carrying a dead body for cremation, sighting him is believed to minimise the inauspiciousness of the death and is, therefore, welcome. The unexpected arrival of a renouncer (*sannyāsī*) at a *vidyāramba* (beginning of the study of the sacred texts) ceremony is highly auspicious but the encounter of a marriage party with him is equally highly inauspicious and, therefore, dreaded. To take a final example, the Brahmans in both Kashmir and Uttar Pradesh consider milk as one of the purest drinks and one that is consumed on auspicious occasions as also offered in worship to deities. It is, however, never consumed at the commencement of a journey for which occasion yoghourt is the appropriate food item, though it may not be offered to a deity.

The nature of the priest, the Mahābrahman and the renouncer, or of milk and yoghourt, does not change but the significance of different events alters one's relationship to these persons and foods as the normal (not necessarily desirable) life trajectories of the actors involved in them are, as it were, reinforced or deflected and weakened. These examples point to the 'heterogeneousness of time' (Eliade 1974:147); and the consequent perplexities of the mind in the face of inauspiciousness. The anxiety, fear and emotional disturbance which ominous events give rise to are, according to my informants, much more intense than the doubts regarding correct conduct associated with the contact with impure persons, objects and places: my own observation of people's behaviour in rural Kashmir confirms this assertion.

III

Concerning the category 'śubha' and 'śuddha': ethnographic notes and queries

I now turn to ethnography to explore how the notion of auspiciousness has been handled by anthropologists. I will not undertake a comprehensive survey of literature but confine myself to three authors, namely M. N. Srinivas, R. S. Khare and Frédérique Marglin, each one of whom has devoted considerable attention to this subject, to point out some critical issues that seem to be worthy of clarification and further research.[15]

In his classic study of religion and society among the Coorgs of south India, Srinivas (1952) went into the details of purity and pollution with unprecedented care and also made an important contribution to our understanding of auspiciousness as an aspect of domestic life. It would seem that his earlier study of marriage and the family among various castes of Karnataka, based on his own fieldwork and on published works (see Srinivas 1942), had already sensitised him to this important cultural notion among Hindus. He had thus noted that purchases for a marriage are made and the marriage solemnised on an auspicious day and that married women—the so-called *sumaṅgali*—are particularly qualified to bless a bride (*ibid.*: 68-75).

In his second book, Srinivas points out quite early that, according to Coorg belief, 'Every important task must begin in an auspicious moment, or it will fail' (1952:39). He then dwells on the ritual of *maṅgala* or auspiciousness (ibid.:70ff.), which may be performed on certain happy occasions in the life of an individual but is specifically identified with marriage. *Maṅgala* is described by him as 'an auspicious or good-sacred ceremony that has to be performed on an auspicious day' (*ibid.*:74); the central rite of *mūrta* (derived from the Sanskrit *muhūrta*) in the *maṅgala* complex is performed during a particularly auspicious part of the chosen day. Moreover, the ritual is performed in an auspicious place such as the ancestral home. *Maṅgala* results in a rearrangement of social structure dramatised by the change in the status of the nubile girl who now becomes a *sumaṅgali*, that is one who has a beneficent influence on the lives of other people, obviously by virtue of being herself a blessed person (*ibid.*:157).[16] It follows that a widow, who must live alone and not in the conjugal bond,[17] has lost her own blessedness as well as the power to bless.

All this fits in well with the analysis in the previous section of this essay, but it has to be noted that Srinivas does not bring out as clearly as one would have wished the various nuances of meaning in the different uses of the word 'auspicious'. His use of it as a general adjective which defines events, persons and places alike may conceal the fact that in its primary connotation the word refers to an event—to marriage—which produces general well-being (literally, *maṅgala* in Sanskrit). What is perhaps even more regrettable is his decision to include auspiciousness and purity together in the encompassing category of 'good-sacred' without clearly distinguishing between them. He also draws attention to certain formal similarities between actions characteristic of auspicious and inauspicious occasions without providing us with a discussion of the significance of this formal similarity and of the content of these actions. That 'inversion' occurs is, however, quite obvious.

Commenting on Srinivas's handling of *maṅgala*, Dumont and Pocock (1959:33) suggest a deeper structure by assimilating auspiciousness into what they consider to be the most fundamental of underlying ideas, namely purity. I do not find this way of resolving the problem of the relationship between auspiciousness and purity quite satisfactory as it ignores the need to examine the independent character of the relations of auspiciousness. The crucial observation in this regard, it may be recalled from the previous section of this essay, is that there are no empirical examples available of the combination of the inauspicious and the pure in a single event though the other three combinations are exemplified by birth (auspicious-impure), death (inauspicious-impure) and marriage (auspicious-pure)—a fact noted by these authors themselves (though not exactly in the same terms as employed here). Their position is, ultimately, derived from their premise that 'the religion of caste is fundamental' (*ibid.*:34).

I now turn to Khare's two books on the cultural significance of food among the Kānyakubja Brahmans of Uttar Pradesh (north India) in which he employs the words 'auspicious' and 'inauspicious' quite extensively. His most general definition of auspiciousness is in terms of those regular happenings which symbolise or seek to bring about a 'pervasive, established domestic value' of collective and comprehensive well-being (1976a: 109, 121n, 185, *et passim*). He clearly sees purity as a value encompassed by the value of auspiciousness. He writes: 'All regular ritual techniques that help establish ritual purity ultimately result in a Hindu householder's constant concern with a morally desirable auspiciousness (for there is no other kind) which, for him, must pervade the ritual and social world if everything between him, his social groups and his gods is proceeding properly' (*ibid.*:109). Elsewhere, he writes that irrespective of the states of purity and impurity, 'the inauspicious (*aśubha*) should not be allowed to take over in one's household life' (*ibid.*:144).

In view of the foregoing, it is rather surprising that Khare should not have maintained clearly and consistently the distinction between auspiciousness and purity—between events and things—and should have merely written of the 'congruence' between the two (1976b:71f): the equation that he sets up ('auspiciousness: pure: high:: inauspiciousness: impure: low') breaks down as—to repeat—birth is an auspicious event but causes pollution. A further blurring of heuristically important distinctions occurs when Khare (like many other scholars) prefixes the adjective 'auspicious' to foods, food areas, cooking utensils, food processing implements, cooking techniques, and even numbers without bringing out clearly the temporal context. It is, however, only fair to acknowledge that he does draw attention to the character of some objects (such as utensils) as 'definite and dominant symbols of happiness and sorrow' (*ibid.*:55) and also points out that certain actions (for example, certain cooking techniques) are similarly symbolic of 'normalcy or auspiciousness or festivity' (*ibid.*:62). This is the familiar relation between the signifier and the signified and should be elaborated in future research on the subject.

The third scholar whose work I discuss here is Frédérique Marglin. Her primary concern is with the role of the king and of the *devadāsīs* in the ritual complex associated with the Jagannātha temple at Puri. She pursues her studies along several thematic paths, including notably a richly documented and explicitly articulated discussion of the nature and significance of auspiciousness, purity and power (*śakti*). It is not possible here to undertake a detailed exmination of her published and unpublished work (1977, 1978, 1980,

1982) and I will confine myself to drawing attention to the following aspects of it.

(1) Marglin makes a clear distinction between auspiciousness and purity: the latter is said to pertain to the ordered, hierarchical domain of caste but the former is free flowing. This is best exemplified by the fact that, though the *devadāsīs* are associated with auspiciousness in diverse ways—they dance and sing in the temple everyday and on various special occasions; they also sing the joyous songs of well-being (*maṅgalagīta*) in the homes of their patrons (the priests of the temple) on happy occasions connected with the lifecycle, most notably marriage—and though they are unfettered by caste regulations, yet they are not allowed to go into the inner sanctum of the temple because they are considered unchaste. Their auspiciousness arises from their being the wives of the god Jagannātha and his representative on the earth, the king of Puri; they are *ahya*, ever-married for the god transcends the mortal domain of birth and death. The *devadāsīs*' impurity results from their being permitted (in fact, expected) to live as concubines of the temple priests who are the servants (*sebāka*) of the god. Their body (*deha*) is, therefore, impure. This essential distinction between auspiciousness/inauspiciousness and purity/impurity (to which I have already drawn attention in the discussion of everyday usages earlier in this essay) thus seems to be supported by empirical evidence from different domains of life and also analytically illuminating.

(2) Marglin also presents a list of the cultural meanings, embodiments and 'representatives'—the signifiers—of auspiciousness. It is said to refer to a state of well-being, happiness and pleasure. It is associated with eating and the plentifulness of food; with sexual union, fertility and growth; with progeny and prosperity. It is embodied in, or represented by, water jars, aquatic animals, flags, doors, erotic sculptures, sounds, etc., and, above all, the *devadāsīs*. They are called by Marglin the 'harbingers of auspiciousness'; she also designates them as the 'specialists in auspiciousness'.

When Marglin refers to *devadāsīs* as specialists in auspiciousness (and the tribal *daitā* as specialists in inauspiciousness), I take it to mean that, though what the *devadāsīs*/*daitās* do has happy consequences because their works are ultimately conducive to well-being (*maṅgalakārya*), yet there are elements in the situation in which the *daitās* are involved which are inauspicious, namely, the illness and the 'death' of the gods. However, the rejuvenation of the gods also begins at the hands of the *daitās*. The element of the passage of time is important here and, as Marglin illustrates richly, the Hindu conception of it may be more complex than what would be familiar from a Western perspective. Thus while auspiciousness and the *devadāsīs* are said to symbolise the forward flow of time—the present in relation to the future—inauspiciousness and the *daitās* are related to the reversal of time, that is death and the past. The *daitās* seem to be of crucial significance as they dramatise the flux of time more sharply than do the *devadāsīs* so much so that the demarcation between auspiciousness and inauspiciousness itself appears to be arbitrary or is resolved. Marglin does not, however, push her analysis in this direction.

It would be useful to recall here two important distinctions mentioned by me earlier: first, between objects and persons *as such*, on the one hand, and these as symbols, on the other; second, between objects and persons, on the one hand, and events and performances on the other. When the *devadāsīs* are called *maṅgalanārī* or the songs they sing, *maṅgalagīta*, it is clear that two meanings are implied: first, and obviously (even superficially perhaps), these women and their songs contribute to an atmosphere of joy; second, they are associated with happy events whether these occur (births) or are arranged (weddings, pilgrimages). In the process they come to symbolise auspiciousness. Though the distinction between person or act, event and symbol may be blurred in speech and in the minds of speakers, its validity must not be lost sight of by the student.

When pilgrims come to Puri they are told by the priests that seeing and circumambulating *devadāsīs* are auspicious. That is these actions produce well-being. In the same spirit, worshippers in the temple pick the dust from the feet of dancing *devadāsīs*, or roll on the ground where they have danced, in the hope of attaining well-being, of winning divine grace, for they are told that the *devadāsīs* are the embodiment of Lakṣmī.[18] We see here instances of the coalescence of the carrier or bearer of auspiciousness (the *devadāsī*) and its ultimate source (Lakṣmī) and this too should be borne in mind.

(3) This brings me to the third point I want to make. In her analysis of the consecration ritual within the famous Car Festival (*ratha yātrā*) ritual complex, Marglin brings out clearly the interrelatedness of time, place, and person or actor: the *devadāsīs* and the *daitās* are described as doing different things in different parts of the temple on this very special occasion, all contributing to a single though complex task. An actor (*pātra*) in this context, stands for not a merely neutral being but an adept, one worthy of receiving the responsibility for a certain role. The issue is that of establishing *pātratā* that is, one's credentials for the performance of the role. The Brahmans and the *daitās* are born into their role categories; the *devadāsīs* are recruited from different castes for their roles by being dedicated to Jagannātha.

Auspiciousness, then, refers in Marglin's analysis to a situation which enables us to see its constitutive elements in their interrelatedness and thus in the right perspective. The actor or person (*pātra*), motivated by an explicit purpose (*uddeṣya*), and specifically recruited to fulfil it, performs an act or role (*kārya*), in a prescribed manner (*rīti*), in a certain place (*sthāna*) at a specified time (*kāla*), which results in collective well-being (*maṅgala*). That is: the *devadāsī*, dedicated to god, imbued with divine devotion, sings and dances in the outer sanctum of the temple at various times of the day and in the year: and this brings about well-being, just as the feeding of the god by the Brahmans does: and the feeding and the dancing take place simultaneously. Dancing, we are further told, symbolises (stands for) sexual union in this ritual context. If any one of the elements (purpose, properly accredited actor, the action, the time, and the place) is absent or imperfect, though nothing else is changed, formally, the auspiciousness of the situation disappears. To illustrate, the most talented Oḍissi dancer could not be allowed to dance in the temple for she is not the right *pātra*, just as the *devadāsī* may not leave Puri to become a professional dancer and yet retain the right to participate in the ritual complex of the temple for she would have violated the parameters of time and place and abandoned the legitimate purpose of her work. Needless to add, what is true of the *devadāsī* is also applicable to the Brahman and the *daitā*.

The 'situation', I may add, must be conceptualised in dynamic rather than static terms: it must be seen as an event, a point which I emphasised earlier in this essay in the course of my examination of the everyday usage of the words *śubha* and *śuddha*. Time is thus the key element in the situation which illumines the others. In this context the observations of two Uttar Pradeshi Brahman informants—both pundits of the traditional type—appear to be apposite. According to them, *kāla* is the ultimate cause of everything that happens. Its characteristic manifestation is *pravāha* (flow) or *vartana* (movement, circular movement). It is *anādi* (without beginning), *ananta* (without end) and *sarvavyāpaka* (all-pervading, encompassing). Deified as Kāla, it is the guardian of life and the upholder of *dharma* (righteousness). It is not amenable to human control. *Deśa* or *sthāna* (place, location), the informants maintained, is *vyāpya* (permeable, encompassed): it has been created and will be destroyed in time. Human beings realise their being within this framework, in the union of *śakti* and *prakṛti*.[19]

IV

Concluding Remarks

J. L. Austin once complained that the history of Western philosophy was littered with 'tidy-looking dichotomies' with the student being required to embrace one half or the other (1962:3). It certainly has not been my intention to propose oversimplifications of this type in respect of the categories *śubha* and *śuddha* in Hindu culture. I have only tried to suggest that certain analytical distinctions are heuristically useful inasmuch as they enable us to understand better the relations and the principles of relationship between the categories under examination.

If auspiciousness/inauspiciousness refers primarily to events—and ultimately to life itself as an event-structure—and if purity/impurity is basically an attribute of objects, why have anthropologists confused the categories by objectifying the events? It would seem that this has happened because we have tended to follow too closely what the informants say. Though the informants are usually well-aware of behavioural norms and everyday usages, they are not always aware of ambiguities in these. Moreover, they readily—almost unthinkingly—switch from literal to figurative language and back again. In other words, they speak in metaphors, carrying over aspects of events (or objects) to objects (or other objects), and also ignoring the distinction between mental and physical concepts—between words and things. Auspicious married women and inauspicious widows are instances of the transferred epithet (see Lakoff and Johnson 1980). Our task as anthropologists would seem to lie in overcoming ambiguity and decoding figurative language and bringing out clearly what we receive through interrogation and observation confusedly. We seek to abstract certain concepts in a cross-cultural framework that hardly concern the people whose culture we study and, therefore, remain inarticulated and unexpressed in it. Auspiciousness is highly meaningful to people in their everyday life but the abstract concept of the passage of time is much less so. Our own hesitation to explicate such concepts, however, leads us to draw conclusions too soon and at too low a level of generality to produce better understanding.

The present essay, then, points to the need to explore more systematically than has been done heretofore the relatively neglected theme of auspiciousness/inauspiciousness in Hindu culture. This should not be done, of course, independent of the notion of purity/impurity—for then we would produce only distortions of reality—but in relation to it. The particular expressions and associations of the notion of auspiciousness may vary but it is quite clear that it is of basic importance at least in the scheme of values of upper castes and is associated with the passage or flux of time and the significance of this fact for human life. If this notion is found closely interlinked with that of purity among upper castes but wanes as we move down the ladder, that itself would far from downgrading the importance of studying it underscore its potential for deepening our understanding of purity and of the basic elements of Hindu culture.

NOTES

1 R. S. Khare has raised the question whether the idea of auspiciousness is like ritual purity 'a monopoly of the twice born' (1976a: 121n). Louis Dumont in a comment on an earlier draft of the present paper wrote that the Kallar of Tamilnadu, the subcaste of which he made an intensive study, are little concerned with astrological matters; he suggested that auspiciousness is a Brahmanical idea, implying that it is not of the same general importance as purity and pollution. G. S. Bhatt, who has devoted many years to the study of the scheduled castes such as the Camars in Uttar Pradesh, informs me that low castes do entertain beliefs with regard to auspiciousness/inauspiciousness and consult astrologers on such matters as the performance of life cycle rituals. This perhaps points to the deeper inroads of the ideas and behaviour of upper castes into the lives of lower castes in north India as compared to south India.

Bh. Krishnamurthy, the well-known linguist of Osmania University, who also read an earlier draft of this paper, writes (in a personal communication): 'Most of the practices and beliefs described in the article have counterparts in the Dravidian languages area. It would be interesting to sort out how many of these had their origin in native (folk) cultures of India cutting across the caste system and how many are prevalent only in the higher castes. I am thinking of, for example, *śubha nakṣatra* which is a part of the religious observances of upper castes as opposed to *śubha śakuna* which is prevalent in many communities including tribals.' It is obvious that we need more ethnographic data on this subject than we have now to answer these (and other) questions.

2 To elaborate this point, the Fathers at the Delhi Jesuit seminary Vidyājyoti assured me in the course of a discussion (in 1980) that the word 'auspiciousness' has no standard use in their language other than in reference to the 'superstitions' of pre-Christian European peoples and of non-Christians generally. No comment is necessary. As for 'purity,' I know from my fieldwork in the Kashmir Valley that the brahmanical notion of *śuddha* and the

Islamic idea of *pāk*, both rendered into English as 'pure' or 'purity,' for no other appropriate words seem to be available, differ significantly in their connotation. Thus, the *pāk* cooked food of the Muslim is totally unacceptable to the Brahman because it is incurably polluting. Similarly, no good Muslim eats food which has come out of a Hindu kitchen; it is simply *harām*, forbidden.

A disclaimer is, perhaps, called for immediately lest I should be misunderstood to be retreating behind a curtain of Sanskrit words (or words from other Indian languages) into a naive cultural relativism. I remember Goethe's admonition that so long as we know no foreign language we are in a sense ignorant of our own. Comparison is, indeed, the foundation on which anthropology—our knowledge, understanding and evaluation of human cultures through mutual interpretation—is based. In short, all I am trying to do is to argue that direct (surface) translation from one language to another far from contributing to our general understanding of cultural constructs in fact often hinders them.

3 The data for this paper are drawn from the following main sources. (i) My efforts, now extended over many years, to interpret various aspects of the way of life of Kashmiri Brahmans by interrogation and observation (including fieldwork in a village). (ii) Recent conversations with several Uttar Pradeshi (Caturvedī, Kānyakubja and Saryūpārī) Brahmans of Kanpur and Lucknow on the specific theme of this paper. (iii) A few selected ethnographic works.

4 It is worth noting here that one of the secondary meanings of the word *saṅgama* is sexual union which is thus regarded as being comparable to the merger or rivers and similarly auspicious.

5 As is well known to students of classical texts, the contents of the *kalaṣa* vary with the occasion. Thus the contents of the vessel at the coronation ceremony of Hindu kings included the water of many rivers, earth from many places and dwellings, jewels, medicinal herbs, etc. 'The *pūrṇa kumbha* (*kalaṣa ghaṭa*) is, minimally, a pot filled with water, with green leaves from fruit bearing trees, especially mango leaves, covering its mouth, and a coconut placed on top. The pot, placed on white raw rice, is the most wiedely used sign of auspiciousness (*maṅgala*, *śubha*)' (Marglin 1982:161).

6 The fact that priests accept 'ominous children' and 'dangerous goods' from their patrons (*yajamāna*) testifies to the belief in their superior capacity to cope with dangerous situations. They thus come to symbolise danger itself. At the same time there is, at least among the Kashmiri Brahmans, a barely concealed deprecation of the priests for the same reasons and hence a sense of inauspiciousness is aroused on encountering them on particular occasions (when, for instance, their services are not required).

7 Bh. Krishnamurthy comments (in a personal communication): '*Śubhanāma* seems to be a recent innovation. There is no corresponding expression in the Southern languages; and there is no antonym, *aśubhanāma*.'

8 According to a Caturvedī Brahman informant, applying the *tilaka* (a very visible mark of auspiciousness) on the forehead produces well-being particularly so if this is done with the thumb of the right hand (the Kashmiri Brahmans use the middle finger) and the thumb has *śubhalakṣana* on it.

9 The distinction between *ādhyātmika* or *paramārthika* and *vyavahārika* was made by some Uttar Pradeshi informants as also by R. S. Khare (in a personal communication) who has written extensively on the Kānyakubja Brahmans (see Khare 1976a and 1976b).

10 A Saryūpārī Brahman informant, who is a pundit and an astrologer, told me that he would not hesitate to speak of a *śuddha* moment of time from the point of view of the natural occurence of an event or of a performance. Commenting on this, Baidyanath Saraswati writes (in a personal communication): 'Based on astrological calculation, a particular period, ranging from five to ten days or so, is called *śuddha* when the famous "marriage mart" of the Maithil Brahmans takes place and marriages are solemnised. Within that period there are, of course, specific moments of time considered *śubha* for the ceremony. The duration of the *aśuddha* period from the point of view of marriage—called *aticara*—may be very much longer lasting two to three years.'

In this connection, I may point out that one informant pointed out that the horoscope of the Buddha contained the perfect conjunction (*yoga*) of *graha* and thus the *purity* of his Being also embodied the *auspiciousness* of Time.

11 The seven blades of *darbha* are taken as representing the five senses (*prāṇa*), mind (*mana*) and intellect (*budhi*). As the *pavitra* is put on the finger, a Sanskrit *mantra* is chanted: 'You (*pavitra*) are a hundred times purifier of the earth; you are a thousand times purifier of gods; you are health bestowing: I associate you with progeny so that they become rich and abundant in wealth and prosperity.'

12 Kashmiri Brahmans maintain that the highest knowledge, namely the true understanding of *brahmaṇa* (*brahma-gyāna*), has been distilled, as it were, in the Gayatri *mantra*. It is a prayer to the all-pervading Supreme Deity to bless the devotee with *dhī* or higher intelligence for the attainment of such knowledge. The prayer occurs in the Ṛg Veda (III.62.10) as also in the Sāma and Yajur Vedas.

13 Apropos pollution by contact, cf.: 'In this limited sense, impurity is more powerful than purity, but contact here loses something of its religious character: *it does not bring misfortune or disease but only social degradation* (Dumont and Pocock 1959: 30, emphasis added). This is precisely how, I think, the Kashmiri Brahmans also interpret pollution. It should, however, be noted here that some scholars consider this a narrow interpretation: for instance Das (1977) considers the life/death framework more fundamental and inclusive than the pure/impure or the good-sacred/bad-sacred frameworks. She observes: '...the symbolism of impurity marks off situations which are liminal in the sense that the individual experiences his social world as separated from the cosmic. The paradigm for liminality is provided by death...' (*ibid.*:120).

14 See footnote 6 above. Other bad omens recognised by Kashmiri Brahmans include, besides death (particularly during the *pancaka*), unpleasant dreams, the hooting of owls (symbolising death and destruction), etc. In Uttar Pradesh the sight of mating crows also is considered a portent of many deaths for crows are identified with ancestors.

15 I should mention here that I find the absence of any discussion of the category of auspiciousness in my account of family and kinship among the Pandits or rural Kashmir (see Madan 1965) rather disconcerting though not inexplicable. I did mention auspiciousness and did not confuse it with purity but did not distinguish between events (weddings) and persons (sons). I also failed to clarify that it was not in sons as such that auspiciousness resides but in what they do—most notably, they feed the manes, beget sons and continue the lineage.

16 In his account of marriages among the Karnataka castes, Srinivas points out that the *tālī*, which the bridegroom ties round the bride's neck, has knots in it made by her mother and other *sumangali* and is threaded by a prostitute who is referred to as *nitya* (ever)-*sumangali* (Srinivas 1942:75). Writing on Tamil Women, Reynolds says that *cumannkali* literally means an auspicious woman but clarifies that this auspiciousness does not refer to her own being as a woman but to her relationship with certain significant 'others', notably her husband and children (1980:38).

17 See footnote 4 above.

18 On being told of this, one of my Kānyakubja Brahman informants recalled the myth of the crocodile who tried to drag an elephant into the river to devour him. Thinking its end had come, the elephant who was a devotee of Viṣṇu, lifted a lotus with its trunk as a last offering to the god. Viṣṇu appeared on the scene and redeemed both the elephant and the crocodile: the former for his pure devotion and the latter because it had touched the foot of a devotee —itself an act of piety.

19 It may be mentioned here that much attention has been devoted to the concepts of *kāla* and *deśa*/*sthāna* in the Hindu tradition from the Vedas onwards through the Brāhmaṇas, Upaniṣads, and Purāṇas and the two great epics (*Mahābhārata* and *Rāmāyaṇa*). The Nyāya-Vaiśeṣika (one of the six systems of Hindu metaphysics) is particularly concerned with these categories (see Bhaduri 1947).

ACKNOWLEDGEMENT

This essay owes its origin to the discussion I had with Frédérique Marglin in December 1978 on her work on the symbolism of kingship and the *devadāsīs*. Subsequently, the first draft of this paper was prepared at her suggestion for presentation to a seminar on auspiciousness held under the auspices of the Conference on Religion in South India held in May 1980 at George Washington University (Washington, D.C.). I am grateful to John Carman and Frédérique Marglin for the invitation to attend the seminar and for their discussion of the paper.

I also owe thanks to a number of colleagues who read the earlier draft of this paper and took the trouble of sending me their comments in writing. Among them I would like to mention particularly the following: Brenda Beck, G. S. Bhatt, Louis Dumont, Shrivatsa Goswami, R. S. Khare, Bh. Krishnamurthy, F. K. Lehman, Baidyanath Saraswati, K. N. Sharma and M. N. Srinivas.

REFERENCES

AUSTIN, J. L.
1962 *Sense and sensibilia.* London: Oxford University Press.

BHADURI, Sudananda
1947 *Studies in nyāya-vaisheshika metaphysics.* Poona: Bhandarkar Oriental Research Institute.

CARMAN, John B.
1974 *The theology of Rāmānuja.* New Haven: Yale University Press.

DAS, Veena
1977 *Structure and cognition: aspects of Hindu caste and ritual.* Delhi: Oxford University Press.

DUMONT, Louis
1970 *Homo hierarchicus: the caste system and its implications.* London: Weidenfeld and Nicolson.

DUMONT, Louis and Pocock, David F.
1959 "Pure and impure." In *Contributions to Indian Sociology* (1959)3: 9-34.

ELIADE, Mircea
1974 *Patterns in comparative religion.* New York: New American Library.

KHARE, R. S.
1976a *The Hindu hearth and home.* New Delhi: Vikas Publishing House.
1976b *Culture and reality: essays on the Hindu system of managing foods.* Simla: Indian Institute of Advanced Study.

LAKOFF, George and Johnson, Mark
1980 *Metaphors we live by.* Chicago: University of Chicago Press.

MADAN, T. N.
1965 *Family and kinship: a study of the Pandits of rural Kashmir.* Bombay: Asia Publishing House.
1975 "Structural implications of marriage in north India: wife-givers and wife-takers among the Pandits of Kashmir." In *Contributions to Indian Sociology*, n.s. (1975)9: 217-44.

MARGLIN, Frédérique Apffel
1977 "Power, purity and pollution: Aspects of the caste system reconsidered." In *Contributions to Indian sociology* n.s. (1977)11,2:245-70.
1978 "Auspiciousness and the devadāsīs." Mimeo of paper presented at the ninth annual workshop of the Conference on Religion in South India, Chambersburg, Penn.

1980 "Wives of the God-King: the Rituals of Hindu Temple Courtesans." Ph.D. dissertation, Brandeis.

1982 "Kings and wives: the separation of status and royal power." In *Way of life: king, householder and renouncer*, edited by T. N. Madan, pp. 155-81. New Delhi: Vikas Publishing House.

MONIER-WILLIAMS, M.

1976 *A Sanskrit-English dictionary.* Delhi: Motilal Banarsidass.

REYNOLDS, Holly Baker

1980 "The auspicious married woman." In *The powers of Tamil women*, edited by Susan S. Wadley. Syracuse: Syracuse University.

SRINIVAS, M. N.

1942 *Marriage and Family in Mysore.* Bombay: New Book Co..

1952 *Religion and society among the Coorgs of south India.* Oxford: The Clarendon Press.

Kings and Omens

RONALD INDEN

University of Chicago, Chicago, U.S.A.

I AM TOLD that the ancient Roman Senate would undertake no major venture without consulting a specialist who could interpret the flights of birds and declare whether the outcome would be favorable or not. From the latin verb *spicere*, to look at, and the noun, *avis*, bird, we get our English words auspex (augur or diviner), auspice(s) (omen, approval, support), auspicious (boding well for the future, favorable), and auspiciousness (the state of being favorable). We can say, therefore, that ancient Roman birds are largely responsible for bringing us together here today. Ancient and medieval Indian kings did not differ from the Roman senators in their fascination with omens, portents, wonders, prodigies, signs of all kinds. Needless to say, the only kind of sign that was not important in Hindu classification schemes was the flight of birds. Nonetheless, so that we should not be accused of overlooking the obvious, I will say something about this topic of omens, of auspicious and, mostly, inauspicious signs.[1]

The Sanskrit words which we translate as the adjective "auspicious" are numerous. Some of the more frequent are *maṅgala*, *śubha*, *śiva*, *kalyāṇa*, *śreyas*, *bhadra*, *dhanya*, and *iṣṭa*. These words mean, with varying nuances, pleasant, agreeable, propitious, favorable, salutary, better, fortunate, prosperous, desirable, beautiful, handsome, good, charming, radiant, beneficial, and, yes, auspicious. Each of these terms is employable in a sharply contrasting way with its negative form—*amaṅgala*, *aśubha*, etc.—to mean undesirable, unpleasant, bad, and, of course, inauspicious. Virtually every thing, animal, or person and every occurrence, event, or act can be described in Hindu discourse as one or the other. Most of these terms may also be used substantively to refer to conditions or states. Generally speaking, one tends to see the contrastive pair auspicious/inauspicious associated with other contrastive pairs: gods, *devas*/ancestors, *pitṛs* or gods/anti-gods, *asuras*; day/night; waxing moon/waning moon; north and east/south and west. But the terms of these pairs are accented differently by discursive opponents—death is one thing for a Vaiṣṇava, something else for a Śaiva—and in Indic thought there is nothing inherently auspicious or inauspicious. The sight, for instance, of a pregnant woman inside one's house is auspicious, outside, inauspicious, while the sight of a courtesan/prostitute (*gaṇikā*) out of doors is auspicious, indoors, inauspicious.[2]

The words for auspicious are also used to refer to *signs*, to things seen or heard, which foretell or predict the future occurrence of the state of inauspiciousness or auspiciousness. Finally, these words are used, again adjectivally, to designate the actions, ritual and moral, which bring about the inauspicious or auspicious condition. Apart from cremation, the *saṃskāras*, the so-called life-cycle rites, are examples of *maṅgala* rites, described in detail for the Coorgs nearly thirty years ago by M. N. Srinivas, at the household level.[3]

Kings were, in the theistic discourses of Vaiṣṇavas and Śaivas, those manifestations of Viṣṇu (or devotees of Śiva) who were supposed to bring about the well-being of the countries they ruled; and they were, toward that end, enjoined to engage in daily conduct and in the execution of rituals that were designated as *maṅgala*. So it is no surprise that kings were more than others concerned with auspicious and inauspicious signs. A king had two Brāhmaṇa ritualists with special knowledge of signs, the *purohita*, royal priest, and *sāṃvatsara*, royal astrologer. Hindu ritual texts of the eighth to twelfth centuries, the auspicious period for Hindu kingship, called for a king or, even better, a king of kings, to perform an ensemble of daily, monthly, and annual rites, all of which were stated to be "auspicious" and all of which bristled with divinations.[4]

Every day the king and the royal priest examined the sacrificial fire of the palace for signs.[5] The royal priest was also supposed to look into the king's dreams for signs. The king, at a later point in this early morning rite, gazed at his face in a plate of clarified butter which his *purohita*, again, examined for auspicious and inauspicious signs. If the ghee was clear and sweet-smelling, there would be victory (*vijaya*), if it smelled bad or slipped in the dish, it forebode danger (*bhaya*), and if his face was distorted (*vikṛta*) in it, he would obtain death; if radiantly handsome (*suprabha*), well-being (*śubha*).[6] Before he left his quarters and entered his audience hall, the king also took hold of or touched auspicious articles (*maṅgalālambhana*). These were: a Brahmana, cow, fire, land, white mustard seeds, ghee, *śamī* wood, rice, and barley.[7]

Every month he was to carry out, by way of his priest and astrologer, the image worship (*pūjā*) of the sun, moon, and planets (all referred to by the term, *graha*) and lunar asterisms (*nakṣatras*); and, for six months of the year, he was to undergo a Bath of Growth (*puṣyābhiṣeka*). Once a year a king had to undergo another bath, the anniversary repetition of his Ceremonial Bath into Kingship (*rājyābhiṣeka*). He was also enjoined to perform the honorific worship of Indra's standard, pay homage to a painted image of Durgā, carry out an elaborate Nīrājana ceremony connected with his army, and see to the completion of the most elaborate ceremony performed in his kingdom, the annual procession of the god designated as the "cosmic overlord" in it. On virtually all of these occasions, the king and his ritualists looked for auspicious and, especially, inauspicious signs. Furthermore, certain of these rituals, the worship of the heavenly bodies and the *koṭi-homa*, Oblation of Ten Million, a fire rite attached in at least one text to the god's processional ceremony, were closely tied to the interpretation of omens.

Predictably enough, the occasion when signs were most zealously sought were the annual royal progress, in the course of which a rival king might be faced in battle, and before any such battles themselves took place. If a Vaiṣṇava king saw (or heard) any one of a number of inauspicious things as he stepped through the palace gate, he had to return and worship Viṣṇu. If he saw it again, he did not proceed.[8] Mission aborted. Before any armed contest, royal dreams were incubated, interpreted for signs of victory or defeat. And signs, *śakuna*, of success or failure were sought in relation to the army itself—its men, vehicles, and weapons.

Although these signs of future success or failure with respect to a specific undertaking or person were more likely to be sought out on the occasions I have just specified—indeed, according to the cosmology which makes these omens possible they were more likely to occur at these times—favorable or unfavorable signs pointing to a great diversity of future events could appear in a wide variety of times and places apart from these rituals. Whether they were divined in a ritual setting or they occurred independently, the signs to which the greatest attention appears to have been paid were inauspicious "occurrences" or "events" (*udbhava*). These could be of two kinds, *anukūla*, "with the current" or *anuloma,* "with the grain or hair," that is, favorable, and *pratikūla*, "against the current," or *pratiloma*, "against the grain," that is, unfavorable. Occurrences of the latter variety, those contrary to the cosmomoral order, against nature, were designated by a number of terms—*adbhuta*, that which has occurred or arisen in excess, *utpāta*, an irruption, and *vikāra* or *vaikṛti*, abnormal condition, irregularity, disfigurement. All of these terms can be translated by such English terms as prodigy, marvel, and wonder. These breaches in the normal order of things were also referred to by the terms *nimitta*, *rūpa*, or *pūrvarūpa*, and *lakṣaṇa*, all of which we may render by our words sign, omen, or portent.

Here are some examples of these prodigies and the future events of which they were the signs. There were, as we shall again note, three kinds of irruptions—celestial, atmospheric, and terrestrial. To begin with, celestial omens, potentially the most dangerous:

> A double sun in the sky indicates increase for Kṣatriyas; a double moon, (increase) for the Brāhmaṇas; more than that, however, (indicates) a cosmic retraction (*pralaya*). When the orb of the sun or the moon is red at sunrise or sunset and there are no clouds in the sky, it is a sign of great danger. When the moon is dark brown and ugly as it leaves the lunar mansion of one's birth, one should recognize that disaster (awaits) him. When Rahu delays his appearance or appears for too long, the oppression of subjects by disease, famine, and thieves is to be pointed to.[9]

Atmospheric irregularities were less threatening:

> When it rains blood, there is danger from weapons. As a result of the rain of charcoal and grit/dust (*pāṃsu*), the capital is ruined; (if it rains down) marrow, bones, fat, or flesh there is danger of an epidemic (*janamāra-bhaya*).[10]

Least encompassing in their effects were terrestrial portents:

> Fires afflict that kingdom in which a fire suddenly flares up without fuel or does not catch when it does have fuel.[11]
>
> When animals and birds of the forest enter a village and those of the village enter the forest;

> when those of the water crawl onto the land and those born on dry land violently and fearlessly enter the water; when, moreover, friendly ones do unfriendly things at the royal gate or the entrance to the city; when those of the day, furthermore, roam at night while those of the night move about during the day, it indicates that the people of the village will abandon the village.[12]
>
> When dogs have sticks, fire-brands, bones, and cattle-horns in their mouths and take them from the village to the cremation ground, they announce plague (*māraka*) and bode destruction for even the best of villages.[13]
>
> When a log, wooden spoon, or axe behaves strangely; or, when the tails of cows smack at servants and wives—wherever there is a prodigy on the part of a domestic article (*upaskara*), there is a dread danger of (attack with) weapons.[14]

One last category of unnatural events which, though occurring on earth, were in fact celestial in scope because of their loci:

> Images of gods dance, shoot flames, call out, weep, sweat, or laugh; stand up or sit down, run, and deploy or discard their weapons or flags with their arms; or, they come down (from their pedestals) and wander from place to place or spit out fire, smoke, fat, blood, or brains. Whenever such prodigies are seen with respect to lingas, temples, or pictures (of a god) among Brāhmaṇas, one should not consider it appropriate to remain there. Disaster will strike the king and on account of that, the entire country is destroyed.[15]

Were all of these readings of signs a mass of mindless superstitions based on a misunderstanding of the natural world by men who, because of their ignorance, lived in constant fear of their surroundings, besieged by figments of their prelogical, prescientific minds? Or were they, from a more up-to-date perspective, symptoms of an underlying, unconscious, psychically grounded cultural system, hidden from all but us social scientists with our Archimedean fulcrums of structuralism, semiology, Freudian psychology, phenomenology, and ethnomethodology? Hardly. These signs and their treatment were integral to Vaiṣṇava and Śaiva cosmology and theology, and they were explicitly classified and explained in the texts of this so-called medieval period.

I shall argue here: 1) that auspicious and inauspicious signs and acts are to be understood as features of a world constituted as a hierarchy of masteries, lordships, and overlordships, all of which were supposed to have emanated from an absolute Overlord of the Cosmos; 2) that inauspicious signs predicted the diminishment of a human master's, lord's or overlord's domain, often depicted as female, as his mistress, bride, lover, or wife, which diminution could extend to the destruction of both her and himself; 3) that auspicious signs or, simply, the absence of inauspicious signs, foretold the augmentation of a human master's, lord's or overlord's domain; 4) that inauspicious acts were those that diminished a domain while auspicious ones were those that properly augmented it; 5) that the lordships of this "chain of being" were related to one another by resemblances, visible or invisible; 6) that the minor event constituting the inauspicious sign itself resembled the major event it predicted; 7) and, finally, that knowldge of these resemblances—of which divine lord commanded which things, animals, and people, and of the particular rites to be performed in his (occasionally, her) honor—was the sine qua non for interpreting omens and responding to them.

Incidentally, I will say one word here about purity and acts of purification and then drop the subject. The condition of personal purity (*śuci*) was concerned with the "competence" (*adhikāra*) of a master to act with respect to his domain. Acts of purification increased or restored a person's competency. So, for example, a man temporarily lost his competence to perform rituals and make gifts when his father died, a woman lost her competence to cook during her menstrual period. The relative degrees of purity of persons by caste, gender, and the like, referred to the relative competencies to act with respect to the domain of the "social" whole, historically a kingdom or local cult, to which they belonged. Thus, women and Sudras were, in Brahmanism, impure in relation to the Vedic sacrifice because they did not possess the competence to perform it.

On, now, to the Hindu discourse on prodigies, our source for which is a text attributed to one Garga the Elder and elicited from him by the sage, Atri, who asks him to divulge his knowledge of irruptive portents: "Tell me about the omens (*pūrva-rūpa*) destructive of people of the countryside (*jana*), of the royal capital (*nagara*), and also of kings, for you know about them all."[16] The three units enumerated here are assumed to be in a hierarchic relationship, each one named being progressively included in the next. While the royal capital was the complement of the countryside, the two together making up the kingdom, the former commanded the latter. The royal city also included the countryside in the sense that it was supposed to be a realization of the Hindu cosmomoral order in its entirety whereas the countryside, consisting primarily of lower caste cultivators and small-time merchants, was only a partial and defective realization of the Vaiṣṇava or Śaiva cosmos.

The kingdom constituted by the royal capital and the countryside was, in turn, hierarchically related to the king, the overlord of earth and people, their commander and protector. The king, an earthly realization of the Primordial Man (*puruṣa*), the Cosmic Overlord himself, was thought to include within his persona all of the constituent elements of his kingdom just as the Cosmic Man included the constituent elements of the universe in his.

Back to Garga, who replied as follows to Atri's questions:

> Disaster (*upasarga*) constantly arises as a result of excessive greed (*atilobha*), lying (*asatya*), lack of belief in the gods (*nāstikya*), demerits (*adharma*), and the misconduct (*apacāra*) of men. The misconduct of mortals in turn displeases (*apa-rañj*) the gods. They send forth (*sṛj*) prodigious (*adbhuta*) occurrences (*bhava*) in heaven, in the atmosphere, and on earth. These portents fashioned by the gods (*deva-nirmita*) sally forth (*vi-car*) in order to destroy people of every description (*sarva-loka*) and make themselves known (*saṃ-bodhaya*) by their forms (*rūpa*).

We learn from this concise but crucial statement that prodigies are signs emitted by the gods in response to the immoral acts of men, that they are warnings of disastrous events to follow. The gods in outer space are lords in relation to men on earth. Gods command and protect people and people are supposed to follow the orders of the gods—the protracted and detailed "instructions", *śāstra*, issued by them—and honor their images. People, however, do not always follow these orders, do not properly perform *pūjā*. On earth itself, the king is the overlord of men and they are supposed to follow his orders. When they do not, the king is to punish them, to exercise *daṇḍa* on them. The gods also punish men with the multitude of disasters they send. If kings do their jobs, there is of course no need for the gods to send disasters. But they do not, so the gods intervene. Yet, because the king includes the people and country of his kingdom within his persona, every portent that appears in his kingdom, no matter where, is also a warning to him. And every calamity that occurs in it, no matter who is directly affected, is also a catastrophe for the king. This is why the king, above all others, was concerned with omens in ancient and medieval India.

As already indicated, savants divided portents into three classes, depending on their place of occurrence. Another passage gives examples of these:

> Irregularities (*vaikṛta*) relating to the planets (*graha*, including the sun, moon, comets and eclipses) and stars (*ṛkṣa*, especially the lunar asterisms) are classed as celestial (*divya*). Attend me with regard to those of the atmosphere (*antarikṣa*). A shower of meteors (*ulkā-pāta*) a red glow on the horizon (*diśāṃ dāha*), a halo around the sun or moon (*pariveṣa*), the City of Celestial Musicians (*gandharva-nagara*, Aurora Borealis), and irregular rain, such-like in this world are designated as atmospheric. Those arising with respect to a mobile or stable creature of the earth, an earthquake originating in the earth, or an unnatural phenomenon (*vaikṛtya*) relating to bodies of water are called terrestrial.

These three realms were also hierarchically related. That is, the lords of heaven, manifest in the stars and planets, were also the lords of the atmosphere and of the earth herself. Consequently, Garga is able to state that,

> The terrestrial type (of portent) is to be recognized as having a minor result and it ripens (*vi-pac*) slowly; that of the atmosphere gives intermediate results and bestows its fruit in a moderate portion of time; the celestial type has a violent/severe (*tīvra*) result and comes quickly as well.

The superiority of the lords of the celestial domain was such that the sign one of them transmitted could portend the destruction not of an ordinary householder or even a village or two, but of whole constituents of a kingdom, eight of which are enumerated:

> It has consequences in the body of the king, the populace (*loka*), the capital (*pura*), the queen (*dāra*), the royal priest (*purohita*), the king's sons, the treasury/revenue (*kośa*), and his vehicles (*vāhana*).

The prodigies of the atmosphere and the earth could affect one or the other of these constituents, but apparently only those of heaven could afflict all of them. Celestial portents could, furthermore, signal disaster not only for a king and his country, but for a whole quarter of the earth (each of which contained seven countries), that is, for an entire empire. The prodigies of heaven could even forecast the destruction of the entire earth toward the end of a cosmic cycle.

How was a king supposed to respond to a portent? Each and every marvel or prodigy was a rupture or reversal of order in the visible domain of an invisible, divine lord. In order to prevent the disaster it portended, the king was supposed to determine which lord was responsible for the omen and perform an auspicious ritual of the *śānti* type. The king made this determination not by way of knowledge that derives from observations but by virtue of the privileged knowledge handed down by the gods to the sages, to Garga the Elder, and to the Brāhmaṇa ritualists at his court:

> Brāhmaṇas expert in the *śāstras* and filled with confidence in the gods (*śraddhā*) examine (*paś*) them with the eye of knowledge (*jñāna-cakṣus*) and explain them to men for their benefit. Made known by the Brāhmaṇas, men with confidence in the gods perform auspicious rites (*maṅgala*) for their pacification (*śānti*) and do not go down to defeat; but those without confidence in the gods who do not perform the rite, either out of an absence of belief in the gods or anger at them, soon perish.

The term *śānti*, from the verbal root *śam*, means to still, appease, quiet, remove, tranquilize, pacify, extinguish. Rituals having *śānti* as their distinctive purpose and referred to as *śāntika* were the complement of rites designated as *pauṣṭika*, which term derives from the verbal root *puṣ*, meaning to grow, increase, nourish. The former removed or extinguished the offenses, the demerits of oneself that threatened to diminish one's domain as a master, lord, or overlord. The latter rites caused that domain to increase or grow, to realize its completion.

The form of a *śānti* rite was, needless to say, complex. Suffice it to say here that it involved the polite "honoring" (*pūjā*) of a properly installed image of the divine lord who had caused the prodigy to occur, praise of him with appropriate mantras, and the offering of tribute, *bali*, consisting of food and other articles favored by him and resembling him in form and substance. It always included a *homa*, oblations of ghee into a fire—the mouth of the gods—which were carried by the smoke to the sky-dwelling gods. By thus showing his awareness of the divine lord's lordship, and of the offense that had displeased him, by honoring him in this way, the king (or other sacrificer) removed or stilled the offense he had committed, cancelled the demerit he had accrued. Pleased by this honorific treatment and the awareness it entailed, the divine lord then decided not to order the disaster portended by the prodigy he had caused.

Four of the rites regularly performed by the king, and mentioned above, were themselves *śānti* rites. The image worship of the planets and stars was, of course, the most important of these, dealing with the lords of outer space. The *koṭi-homa*, Oblation of Ten Million, was a variant of this apparently meant to cancel offenses and portents that occurred in the rainy season. The Nirajana removed defects implanted in the men, animals, and weapons of the royal army. The Bath of Growth (*puṣyābhiṣeka*) dealt primarily with portents of the atmosphere outside the rainy season.

There were still other rites, called *mahāśanti*, "great" *śānti* ceremonies, designed for performances on specific occasions. Our expert in divination, Garga, is said to have enumerated no less than twenty-one forms of this rite. Three of them, the Saumyā, Abhayā, and Amṛtā could be performed after the observation of any portent, though they were also connected with the portents of heaven, the atmosphere, and the earth, respectively. They were especially to be performed by kings who wished to augment their domains but suffered from diminished capacity. These three rites were hierarchically related to one another, in keeping with the degree of the diminished capacity. The rite meant to deal with the disasters emanating from outer space, the Saumyā ("pertaining to the moon," auspicious) was, consistent with the greater, more encompassing power to do harm of these lords, the rite performed by the king whose domain was most reduced. It was the ritual for a king whose body itself was "inauspicious". He wished to perform sacrifices (*yajña-kāma*) but could not because he had contracted that peculiarly royal disease of India, *rājayakṣma*, "royal withering," (possibly some sort of tuberculosis or consumption) or had been "injured" (*kṣata*) or "weakened (*kṣīṇa*), and therefore lacked the competence to perform sacrifices. The Abhayā ("pertaining to the removal of fear") was to be performed by a king whose body was in good condition and who could sacrifice, but whose kingdom—his domain outside his body—was in a bad way. It was overcome by enemies, there was fear that he might have been enchanted by his rivals, or suffered from some great fear (*bhaya*). The Amṛtā ("pertaining to immortality") was to be performed by a king whose body was not afflicted and whose kingdom was not besieged, but who desired to conquer his foes and gain prosperity, good health, and movable wealth. That is, it was to be carried out by a king who wished to augment the domain of which he was lord, to move it towards completion so that he could gain immortality.

The remaining eighteen *mahāśāntis*, each of which was named after the god, the divine lord who was to be honored, were supposed to remove offenses connected with specific prodigies. The text directs the priest to select the one to be performed in accord with criteria which make it very clear that prodigies are events that occur in the domains of the divine lords who command them to happen, and that, in the emanationist, hierarchic world of Śiva and Viṣṇu the portents also resemble their lords. So, when animals (*paśu*) die, or men turn fierce (*dāruṇa*) or ghosts (*bhūta*) appear, one is to perform the Raudrī *śānti* in which Rudra or Śiva, who himself has a fierce temper and appearance and is lord of animals, *paśupati*, and lord of ghosts, *bhūteśvara.* When there was an omen predicting a loss of money (*dhana*), a tree prodigy occurred, or one involving wealth (*artha*), the king was to perform the Kauberī. The god Kubera was the lord of wealth, *artheśvara*, and the bestower of coins, *dhanada*, as well as the lord of tree-sprites, a *yakṣeśvara.*

Signs affecting the king himself were of particular concern since whatever disaster he suffered was bound to have consequences for the kingdom that constituted his domain as an earthly overlord. When a king detected encirclement by his external foes (*paracakra*) or dissension within his own kingdom, he was to carry out the Aindrī; he was also to perform this rite before his ceremonial bath into kingship or in order to kill his enemies. Indra was, of course, the king of the gods. The royal priest was also to perform this rite if the king himself exhibited signs auguring his death:

> Hear from me the signs when the ruin of a king approaches: at first, he is hostile to the Brāhmaṇas, and then he is opposed by the Brāhmaṇas; he is censured (*nind*) by the Brāhmaṇas, and he confiscates the wealth (*sva*) of the Brāhmaṇas. He does not remember what has been done for him and is angered when asked for a favor. He is pleased by criticism but praise gladdens him not; and he causes an unprecedented tax to fall on the people out of greed. When these happen, he (the royal priest/astrologer?) should honor (*arc*) Indra together with his consort; and he should prepare feast-worthy *bali* offerings for the gods; and cows are to be given to the best of Brāhmaṇas as well as land, gold, and images worshipped. Carried out in this way, the offense (*pāpa*) is pacified.[17]

People of the twentieth century live under the hegemony of a world-view that presupposes a fundamental dichotomy between a knowing human subject and a knowable objective world of nature, a cosmos of purely external, unthinking realities. It makes no sense for us to speak of natural events in that world as signs of some intending mind, for our natural world has been stripped all but clean of any motivating intentionality. Events in it take place, we say, in accord with "laws", but these laws are not commands issued with a divine or human purpose in mind. They are statements about observable regularities and not about obedience or its negation, disobedience. Consequently, the ongoing relations between human events and purely natural events (that is, those not brought about by intended human manipulation of nature) are accidental, random, stochastic. Our relations to blizzards, floods, Medfly infestations, forest (or hotel) fires, bridge collapses, eclipses, planetary conjunctions, or airplane and automobile crashes are matters, for us, of chance or luck.

Given this disjunction between moral subject and amoral objective world, it makes even less sense to speak of marvels, wonders, prodigies, or miracles unless we return to that world the concept of an active God, one who is more than a prime mover. For it is simply not possible in the world we have constructed for our natural events to "disobey" their laws. Those laws are our laws, based on our "observation" of the events. If there is a discrepancy between law and "correctly" observed event, it is the laws which have disobeyed the events and the laws which must be rewritten. There are no expiations for sunspots in our cosmology.

The natural world of ancient and medieval India was person-based, constructed by a Cosmic Overlord out of himself. It consisted of a hierarchy of domains each under the command of its appropriate lord. This was a world greater than the human world but continuous with it. In that world all events, whether natural or human, were actions. They were, as Collingwood puts it, events that had both an inside, thought, and an outside, observable behavior.[18] The laws of nature here were orders or commands which could be obeyed or disobeyed. Natural events occurred in India because the gods in charge of the various departments of nature thought they should happen and made them happen—lesser beings or entities were continually made or caused to act on the command of higher ones, as every student of an Indic language knows. That a science of natural events as auspicious and inauspicious signs should emerge in this world not only makes sense. It was a necessity. The laws of that world were not rewritten if they failed to conform to behavior. No, the Indic world had no norms: those who disobeyed the laws were warned with portents and if they did not cancel or expiate their misdeeds, they were punished with disasters.

Human and natural events were, moreover, never in an accidental or chance relationship to one another. They were part of a complex dialogue between men and gods in which unwanted natural events—floods, plagues, infestations, fires, and the like were always responses by the gods to human acts of disobedience. A man ignorant of the science of signs might not know the reason for his affliction or what to do about it, but the reason was there nonetheless.

One last point. Natural events occurred in a regular, predictable manner in the Indic view not because nature was assumed to possess an inherent nisus toward regularity. That is our view. Indic events occurred because the gods in their own domains ordered them to take place in a regular way for the benefit of men and women. The gods (and goddesses, too) could easily change the commands which they issued to their subordinates. Those contraventions, those events going against the grain, the prodigies and portents on which we have focused here, were the most dramatic and conspicuous warnings a deity could send to a king or country, a village or household, of his (or her) displeasure.

NOTES

1 A. M. Esnoul, "La divination dans l'Inde," *La Divination*, ed. André Caquot and Marcel Leibovici (Paris: Presses universitaires de France, 1968), I, 115-139, introduces the topic. More specific is the introduction of D. J. Kohlbrugge, *Atharvaveda-Pariśiṣṭa über Omina* (Wageningen: Veenman and Zonen, 1938), pp. 1-19, and the translations and particularly the notes. Of interest also are B. R. Modak, "Omens and Portents in Atharvan Literature," *Journal of the Karnatak University—Humanities*, XIX (1975), 17-22, and his "Celestial Omens," *ibid.*, XXI (1977), 19-29.

2 *Matsya Purāṇa*, ed. by pandits of the Ānandāśrama (Poona: Ānandāśrama Press, 1907; Ānandāśrama Series, 54) 243.7-20.

3 M. N. Srinivas, *Religion and Society Among the Coorgs of South India* (Oxford: Clarendon, 1952), pp. 70-100.

4 The main source on which I draw here and subsequently is the *Viṣṇudharmottara Purāṇa* (Bombay: Śrīveṅkaṭeśvara Steam Press, 1912), abbreviated below as VDhP. For the royal rites, see VDhP II.152.

5 VDhP II.151.

6 VDhP. II.151.11b-13b.

7 *Atharvaṇa-pariśiṣṭa*, ed. George Melville Bolling and Julius von Negelein (Leipzig: O. Harrassowitz, 1909-10) 4.1.21-24.

8 VDhP II.163.16-17.

9 VDhP I.85.29b-33a.

10 VDhP II.138.3-4a.

11 VDhP II.136.1.

12 VDhP II.143.1-3.

13 VDhP II.143.9b-10a.

14 VDhP II.142.3b-4.

15 VDhP II.135.1-5a.

16 The text of Garga from which I have translated here and on the next three pages is edited from versions in VDhP II.134.1-13, *Matsya Purāṇa* 229.1-13, and the *Vivṛti* of Bhaṭṭotpala on Varāhamihira, *Bṛhat-saṃhitā*, ed. Avadhavivhari Tripathi (Varanasi: Varanaseya Sanskrit Vishvavidyalaya, 1968) 45.1-7. Most of the previous passages were also taken from the text of Garga.

17 VDhP II.144.14-18.

18 R. G. Collingwood, *The Idea of History* (New York: Oxford University Press, Galaxy, 1956), pp. 213-217.

Purity and Auspiciousness in the Sanskrit Epics

ALF HILTEBEITEL

The George Washington University, Washington DC, USA.

THE TWO INDIAN EPICS, the *Mahābhārata* and *Rāmāyaṇa*, are thoroughly familiar with the two different domains of classification: purity-impurity and auspiciousness-inauspiciousness.[1] On occasion, either can be found as the focus of a rather extended independent treatment, as for instance Karṇa's lengthy tirade against the impure (*aśauca*) practices of the Madras, the subjects of king Śalya (*Mbh.* 8.27.66-73 and 8.30),[2] or typical lists of *maṅgalas*, auspicious things, such as the twelve which Yudhiṣṭhira touches when he wakes up on the battlefield, including garlands, well-adorned auspicious maidens (*svalaṃkṛtāh śubhāh kanyā*), and auspicious birds (*maṅgalyān pakṣiṇaḥ*; *Mbh.* 7.58.19-21). One also finds in both epics, but especially in the *Rāmāyaṇa*, frequent references to auspicious and inauspicious omens (*śakunas*) that preview a warrior's performance in battle, reunion with a loved one, or some other eventuality. There is some considerable documentation and discussion of such lists of the pure-impure and auspicious-inauspicious in P. V. Kane's *History of Dharmaśāstra*, with useful references to epic and other classical sources, so I refrain from discussing them further other than to note that Varahamihira in his *Yogayātra* mentions dishevelled hair as inauspicious, a point I will return to shortly.[3]

The two epics do not, however, always treat these two domains of classification differentially. Many episodes highlight both, and bring their relation to each other into strong relief. In doing so, the epics provide important evidence for their study, for they portray their interplay in a fluid narrative form. It will thus be less useful to extract passages, like the one just cited, dealing with either matter alone, than to observe the ways the epics treat purity and auspiciousness in the round. This will involve keeping two things in mind. First, although we may take the terms *śuddha* and *śubha* as corresponding to our basic pair purity and auspiciousness respectively, we must be attentive to larger term-clusters and conceptual frameworks for each of the two domains.[4] Secondly, these two domains cannot be studied satisfactorily in isolation from other domains. It will be useful to pose the question in terms similar to those of R. S. Khare, who insists that an adequate discussion of Indian food preparation must involve recognition of an interplay between four "axes": not only the pure and impure and the auspicious and inauspicious, but the high and the low and festivity and mourning.[5] I will continue to follow the terminology of Dan Sperber and refer to such "axes" as "domains"[6]: thus the domains of purity and auspiciousness. But the epics are like food production in that their use of the symbolism of these two domains involves a convergence with the "vertical" and "ceremonial" domains which Khare cites, as also with the domain of *dharma.* Altogether, these various domains also evoke, through their convergence, a theological dimension to the epics which I have begun to discuss in other papers.[7]

In focusing primarily on the domains of purity and auspiciousness, this paper will draw in part from the results of these other studies. But it will also afford a chance to view these results against the background of a larger issue that is one of my long-range concerns: the relation between the two epics. The examination of the domains of purity and auspiciousness in the two epics allows us to discuss important areas in which the two narratives show significant thematic rapports. To limit discussion, I will treat only two such areas. They involve matters in which the two epics show important parallels and oppositions: the violations of the heroines Draupadī and Sītā, and the preparations for war. The logic of these choices is evident, for in dealing with women, and with killing and death, we are dealing with two subjects that dominate, perhaps more than any others, the Indian tradition's ruminations on the pure, the impure, the auspicious, and the inauspicious.

First let us deal with the women, Draupadī and Sītā. The discussion of these two heroines' representation of themes connected with purity and auspiciousness can be designed around their portrayal through three symbols: their garments, their hair, and in Sītā's case her jewels. As I have dealt with these symbols elsewhere,[8] a summary must suffice here. In Draupadī's case, the pivotal scene is, of course, the dice match, and the primary symbols are first the hair, and secondly the garments. After Yudhiṣṭhira has reluctantly wagered her as his last stake in the gambling match, she is dragged by her dishevelled hair into the Kaurava men's hall (*sabhā*). Her hair is dishevelled because she is menstruating, and her impurity is accentuated by the revelation that she is wearing but one garment, and that bloodstained (*Mbh.* 2.60.25-32; 70.9)[9] Moreover, she protests that she should not be brought before the men in the *sabhā* during this period of defilement. In this connection she is not only impure but inauspicious.[10]

It is the accentuation on Draupadī's impurity, however, that charges this scene with its great power and impact. But is she really impure? Or, to put it differently, what does this impurity mean? First of all, it is an oversimplification to say that menstrual blood is impure. For the woman, at least, it is purifying and cleansing.[11] Thus the outrage committed upon Draupadī involves an *interruption of her purification.* For a woman to resume her wifely duties and prerogatives, it is, moreover, necessary for her to wash her hair after menstruation and bind it into a braid. It seems clear from the *Mahābhārata* that Draupadī avoids doing this for the thirteen years that begin with this violation at the dice match, and culminate—after her exile with her husbands—in the battle of

Kurukṣetra. But she does not, in the epic, ever declare her intentions to keep her hair thus dishevelled. And there is no mention of her finally binding it up. There is thus neither an explicit vow of dishevelment such as can be traced back to Bhāravi's seventh century *Kirātārjunīya* (3.47);[12] nor is there the further vow, traceable to Bhaṭṭa Nārāyaṇa's eighth century *Veṇīsaṃhāra* and now of pan-Indian popularity, that she would keep her hair unkempt until she could braid it with the blood of her tormentor Duryodhana (or of Duḥśāsana, or in some versions of both). Obviously these variant strands of tradition involve different shadings of the themes of purity and impurity, and one must not be overeager to arrange them into a chronology or geography, as the Sanskrit epic itself seems to evoke, echo, or perhaps anticipate "post"-epic and vernacular traditions.[13] But it is clear enough that the epic presents Draupadi as wilfully undertaking a state of extended symbolic menstrual defilement by continuing to wear her hair loose during her twelve years of exile and her thirteenth year in the ironic disguise of a hairdresser.

We have thus noted one way in which the epic story unfolds from the issue of Draupadī's purity: it is not so much that she is impure, but that her purification is interrupted in a way that requires the destruction of her violators. But there is a direct sequel to the hair-pulling that presents a further development of the purity-impurity theme. This is the famous disrobing scene, in which Duḥśāsana attempts to remove Draupadī's garment only to find it miraculously replaced by another, and that in turn by others until he must give up in chagrin. The hair-pulling and the saree-pulling are intimately related symbols, as Bhaṭṭa Nārāyaṇa shows by repeatedly referring to them in a compound: the *keśāmbarākarṣaṇa*, "the pulling of the hair and the garments."[14] But for our purposes, the most significant thing is that Duḥśāsana begins by pulling a garment that, as noted earlier, is bloodstained, and ends up looking at a pile of sarees "of many colors and white" (2.544*).[15] The *Mahābhārata* precedes this miracle with a debate over whether Draupadī is "blameless," "faultless" (*aninditā*) or, due to her polyandry, a "whore" (*bandhakī*; 2.61.23-36), and whether the Kauravas have acted in accord with *dharma* by dragging her into the hall. The miracle of the sarees is clearly an affirmation that she is "blameless," and that her polyandric *dharma* is beyond reproach. These are clearly indications of her essential purity, something which henceforth the epic audience understands even while hearing that she will wear her hair dishevelled and don an impure guise during her period in disguise. For in this period she begins by wearing a "large black very dirty garment" (*vāsas . . . kṛṣṇaṃ sumalinaṃ mahat*; 4.8.2), and she assumes a task that involves handling other peoples' impurity as a hairdresser.[16] The sequence of garments thus bespeaks the symbolisms of purity and auspiciousness: the one blood-stained garment is replaced by garments that are white, an indication of her purity,[17] and multicolored, an indication also of her auspiciousness; and her dirty black disguise is a means of concealing these essentially inviolate qualities.

If we turn now to Vālmīki's portrayal of Sītā, we may note at first that her career parallels Draupadī's in many ways. Each heroine is banished to the forest with her husband(s); each is violated in some fashion by a male; in each case the violation spurs her husband(s) to acts of revenge; and in each case the heroine is restored to queenly status once that revenge is accomplished. Moreover, neither heroine, once restored, retains her queenly status in its full glory. Draupadī is barren due to Aśvatthāman's curse; and Sītā suffers the reproaches of the populace that lead—at least in Vālmīki—to her second banishment, this one by Rāma. It is as if in each case the heroine has been flawed by her earthly encounters. This is part of a larger pattern, found frequently in myths about the Goddess, in which the human forms which the Goddess assumes, and the sufferings she endures, are taken on as penance for some former fault, or in fulfillment of some former vow of revenge. It might thus be formulated that the sufferings of heroines in this world involve a necessary taking on of impurity, conditioned by misfortunes of their previous lives as goddesses or saintly heroines.[18]

Despite such parallel episodes, however, Sītā and Draupadī are in many ways each other's opposites. And it is the symbols of hair, garments, and (with Sītā) jewels that reveal this most clearly.[19] Moreover, the accent in Sītā's portrayal is not so much on the domain of purity as on that of auspiciousness. These contrasts and their symbolic accentuations emerge clearly from the parallel episodes just mentioned in the two heroines' careers.

First of all, although the scenes are similar, the first two occur in a different order. For Draupadī the violation precedes the exile; for Sītā the exile precedes the violation. This is a most significant difference, for whereas Draupadī enters the forest in a state of extended symbolic impurity, Sītā enters the forest with no question about her purity. The main question that concerns Vālmīki is how Sītā can remain with Rāma, despite the reduced circumstances that the forest life will entail, as a *sumaṅgalī*, an "auspicious woman." His answer, in a scene that has comic possibilities, is to first have Daśaratha supply Sītā with enough garments and jewels to last her through her fourteen years of banishment (*Rām.* 2.34.15); and then, toward the beginning of their forest wanderings, to have the saintly Anasuyā supply her with additional accoutrements (2.110.17-20; 111.11-13). No one worries about how this wardrobe is to be carried about. Perhaps it is but another charge of the "fortunate" and ever uncomplaining Lakṣmaṇa. In any case, we are confronted with a heroine who enters the forest with her purity assumed but her auspiciousness doubly guaranteed. She is not disrobed, like Draupadī, but robed to excess.

As to the violations, whereas in Draupadī's case the outrage is focused on her purity, with Sītā the central issue still remains her auspiciousness. While Rāvaṇa bears her away to Laṅkā, she drops her "auspicious" (*śubha*) jewels and her "auspicious" (*śubha*) yellow upper garment to mark the trail of her capture (4.6.9; 5.13.43; 52.2; etc.) so that Rāma will be able to find her. Thus whereas the violation of Draupadī involves a disrobing while she is impure, Sītā's abduction occurs while she is fully auspicious. And while Draupadī's response involves a wilful adoption of the symbolism of impurity to challenge her husbands to revenge, Sītā wilfully uses the symbols of auspiciousness to stimulate Rāma. Most significantly, Sītā retains a vestige of her auspicious finery even during her captivity, and her status during this time is that of a *virahiṇī*—a woman "separated from her husband"—as indicated by the wearing of her hair in a "single braid" (*ekaveṇī*).[20] Here again Sītā contrasts with the dishevelled Draupadī. Moreover, it is with her last jewel that she lets Rāma know of her whereabouts by sending it back with Hanumān for Rāma to see it. It is no accident that this jewel is her *cūḍāmaṇi*, the "crest jewel" with which she fastens her hair and thus indicates what remains of her still auspicious *virahiṇī* status (*Rām.* 5.26.17; 36.52; 63.31; 65.30. etc.).

Further, as to the manner in which the two heroines challenge their husbands, it is significant that Draupadī does so by her constant presence among them. Indeed, she shares her experiences of impurity and defilement with them, as we shall see. Sītā, however, challenges Rāma by her absence, from afar, by speeches conveyed through Hanumān. It is her separation and distance, not her companionship and presence, that is the reproach to Rāma. And Rāma will in no way have to share the impurity which her captivity inevitably entails.

As to their restoration, the *Mahābhārata* is largely silent about Draupadī's reaccession as queen; but it is clear that, even though she is barren, she shares the kingship with her husbands. The impurity she has assumed and the "vows" (*Mbh.* 5.137.18) and *tapas* (9.4.18; 58.10) she has undertaken are fulfilled even if they are not made explicit, and are relegated largely to the past. And from here on she lives out the rest of her life with them. On the contrary, when Sītā is restored to Rāma, and hence eventually to the throne, it is only after she has reluctantly fulfilled Rāma's demand that she appear before him, redeemed from her captivity, only with freshly washed and scented hair and dressed up again in her auspicious finery (6.102.7-13). Here the implicit question of her purity is finally addressed by the "test" which Rāma requires: her entry into the fire. Yet despite her emerging from the fire unscathed, the question of her purity is only partially resolved, relegated not to the past but reserved for the future as a subordinate (and seemingly ambiguous) issue among the deliberations that lead to her second and final banishment. On that occasion, Rāma is convinced that Sītā is "sinless" (*apāpam*; *Rām.* 7.44.6), "of pure conduct" (*śuddhasāmācarā*; 8), and "pure" (*sītāṃ śuddhām*: 9). But the populace doubts this. What is crucial and predominant, however, is Rāma's concern that Sītā be auspicious. It is this concern, and not one for her purity, that leads Rāma to decide on her banishment. Thus he asks his ministers: "'What words, auspicious and inauspicious, do the city folk say? Having heard not, I will do what is auspicious and not what is inauspicious'" (*śubhāśubhāni vakyāni yānyāhuḥ puravāsinaḥ/śrutvedānīṃ śubhaṃ kuryāṃ na kuryām aśubhāni ca*; 7.42.10). Having heard of the people's rumors, the "auspicious" thing he does is to banish his wife, whom he knows to be "pure". Moreover, the text shows its concern for the auspiciousness of the scene by making it clear that Rāma has Sītā escorted into her banishment by "Lakṣmaṇa of auspicious marks" (*lakṣmaṇa śubhalakṣaṇa*; 43.2)—a frequent epithet for Rāma's brother (e.g.

6.79.1) which also reminds us that Rāma is joined in the forest not by just one representative of auspiciousness (Sītā) but two. Finally, Sītā is replaceable in her role as representative of auspiciousness in Rāma's life. After she has died bitterly in her banishment from her husband, Rāma replaces her in rituals by a golden statue (7.82.19).

Our discussion of the heroines thus reveals two different emphases within the two epics. Whereas in the *Mahābhārata* the heroine and the heroes follow a career where their purity and impurity are a central issue, but one which involves them together in an integrated way and includes themes of auspiciousness and inauspiciousness as well, in the *Rāmāyaṇa* the heroine's auspiciousness is revealed as indispensible to the hero. But where the issue of purity is raised, it makes her inauspicious even though she is pure. And the hero must thus repudiate her, his concern for her auspiciousness being more fundamental than his concern for her purity: not his wife's but his own. Whereas the *Mahābhārata* heroes undergo impurity and face inauspiciousness like, and together with, their wife, the hero of the *Rāmāyaṇa* must be kept pure, and surrounded by auspiciousness, at all costs. This contrasting pattern can now be further examined with reference to the foremost heroes of the two epics, Rāma and Arjuna.[21]

Concerning the heroes, one finds further thematizations of the pure, the auspicious and their opposites through symbols of hair and garments. But it is in connection with the wars in each epic that the issues are most intensified. Each epic regards its battle as a sacrifice, and the battles have many sacrificial overtones, including implications—in the *Mahābhārata* at least—that those who are involved in killing take on the impurity of bloodshed like the slaughterer and distributor of portions of the animal in the Vedic sacrifice.[22] Yet the battle, like the sacrifice, also generates purity,[23] and—as Kṛṣṇa teaches Arjuna—killing can be *akliṣṭakarman*, "unstained action," if done without the desire for fruits. In fact, the term *akliṣṭakarman* is used frequently in both epics, and primarily to characterize Rāma and Arjuna.[24] The battles are also full of auspicious and inauspicious augurs, with the battlefield itself suddenly and frequently shifting its aspect, in similes, from a gore-begrimed river of blood to a host of stars on a beautiful moonlit night.[25] Here, however, we will focus not on the wars themselves, but on the preparations for them. In particular, it is prior to the inevitability of death and bloodshed in war that Arjuna and Rāma each undergo a sequence of transformations and interactions that involve them most profoundly with the domains of purity and auspiciousness. We thus turn to Arjuna's disguise, donned during his period of concealment, and Rāma's passage through the hermitage of Matañga to his alliance with the vultures, monkeys, and "bears."[26] Let us anticipate, at the outset, a sort of compensatory pattern. Whereas Draupadī is concerned primarily with purity and secondarily with auspiciousness, Arjuna is concerned primarily with auspiciousness and secondarily with purity. And whereas Sītā is concerned primarily with auspiciousness and secondarily with purity, Rāma is concerned primarily with purity and secondarily with auspiciousness. One can thus chart the accentuation of our two domains in the two epics as follows:

	Mahābhārata primary	secondary		*Rāmāyaṇa* primary	secondary
Draupadī	purity	auspic.	Sītā	auspic.	purity
Arjuna	auspic.	purity	Rāma	purity	auspic.

As Madeleine Biardeau first saw,[27] the year which the Pāṇḍavas spend in disguise is presented in terms of the symbolism of the *dīkṣā*, the "consecration" preparatory to a sacrifice: in this case, the "sacrifice of battle." There are several allusions to the Pāṇḍavas having become like embryos in the womb during this period.[28] The womb-like condition of the *dīkṣā* is thick with associations with danger, death, and impurity,[29] and these affect the Pāṇḍavas and Draupadī alike and in general. Arjuna, in fact, seems most sensitive to such themes when he tells Draupadī of the "unsurpassed" suffering he has experienced while adopting his disguise in the "animal womb" of Matsya, the kingdom whose name means "Fish."[30]

But whereas all the Pāṇḍavas encounter and take on impurity during this period in disguise, Arjuna's disguise—and the activities which it involves him in—are uniquely focused on themes of auspiciousness. Arjuna dons the disguise of a transvestite/eunuch/bisexual named Bṛhannaḍā.[31] As pointed out elsewhere, eunuchs have very ancient functions in India.[32] One of these, appearances at births, can be traced to *Atharvaveda* 8.6. Another function, which might seem more recent until one looks at the evidence for it in the *Mahābhārata*, is to appear at weddings. In both of these circumstances, as well as more generally, there seems little doubt that eunuchs are regarded as impure.[33] But what is interesting is that despite their impurity, their appearances at births and weddings can be either auspicious or inauspicious. They hold the power to bless or curse, and, in today's India, they may bless with song and dance if appropriately paid, or may shower abuse and gesture with obscenities until paid to leave. But even paying for their removal is a way of assuring an auspicious result.

In Arjuna's case, his eunuch role is clearly focused on auspiciousness. This is true even though, as Draupadī tells him, his disguise is one that is "despised by the world" (4.8.11). More particularly, it is as a eunuch that he oversees the auspicious outcome of the wedding and childbirth that result in the sole continuation of the Kaurava-Pāṇḍava line: the marriage of his son Abhimanyu to the Matsya princess Uttarā, and the birth of their son Parikṣit. First, as regards the marriage, it is through his eunuch disguise that Arjuna has access to the royal women's quarters, and particularly to Uttarā. This access enables him to be her instructor in the clearly auspicious arts of song, dance, and music, arts which make her an ideal auspicious bride. And when finally his identity is disclosed and he is offered Uttarā's hand in marriage for himself, it is his eunuch disguise that gives Arjuna the pretext for insisting that Uttarā should marry not himself but his son: their year spent together in asexual intimacy has made her like a daughter to him; moreover, his adopted asexuality is a guarantee of her chastity, and thus of her suitability as a bride for his son.

Secondly, Arjuna the eunuch also prepares Uttarā for her role as a future mother. When he sets off to defend the Kingdom of Matsya against a Kaurava cattle raid, Uttarā asks Arjuna to bring her the Kauravas' garments for her to dress her "dolls" (4.35.23). The garments Arjuna brings back for her are the white robes of Droṇa and Kṛpa, the yellow robes of Karṇa, and the blue ones of Aśvatthāman and Duryodhana (61.13). Once again, as at Draupadī's disrobing, we have multicolored garments that evoke purity (white) and auspiciousness (yellow, blue). It is clear that in dressing her dolls with such garments, Uttarā prefigures her role as a mother-to-be. And the link with Draupadī is intensified by the ambiguity of the term used for dolls. Uttarā asks for the garments *pāñcālikārtham.* This can be rendered "for the sake of (my) dolls," or "for the sake of Draupadī [she who comes from Pañcāla]." The auspicious connotations of the garments which Arjuna the eunuch secures for Uttarā are thus a prefiguration of her becoming the mother of the son who will continue the lineage, a privilege which Draupadī, sonless and barren after the war, must eventually relinquish. Thus the multicolored garments pass, in effect, from Draupadī to Uttarā. And while Uttarā becomes the focus of such auspicious prospects, the garments which Draupadī wears are the impure "dirty black" ones of her hairdresser disguise.

It thus appears that despite the impurity of his eunuch disguise, Arjuna's functions in that role are persistently auspicious: music, song, dance, marriage, and birth.

In the *Rāmāyaṇa*, the preparations for battle which follow upon the abduction of Sītā are filled with equally bizarre encounters, and equally significant evocations of the domains of purity and auspiciousness. It may also be that these encounters can be illuminated by a similar correlation with the theme of the *dīkṣā.* But the *Rāmāyaṇa* has its special twists.

Most of Sītā, Rāma, and Lakṣmaṇa's period of banishment in the forest is a relative idyll. For the better part of their forest tenure, they follow a southward path from one ṛṣi's hermitage to another until they reach that of the last of the great ṛṣis, Agastya, who is associated with the southern boundaries of Aryandom, beyond which Rāma is to meet with sudden disasters. Not surprisingly, their path throughout is described as "auspicious" (*śubhe vartmani*; 6.70.14). But the disasters Rāma encounters once he leaves Agastya's hermitage are indications that in Rāma's career auspicious things sometimes take on strange forms. Not only will Sītā be abducted (something over which the gods and ṛṣis rejoice); Rāma will be guided and accompanied by a bizarre concatenation of pure, impure, auspicious, and inauspicious creatures.

To begin with, once he leaves Agastya's hermitage, he is guided to Pañcavaṭi, where Sītā will be abducted, by the vulture Jatāyus. Not surprisingly, vultures, no matter how friendly, are listed among inauspicious creatures.[34] Then, once Sītā is abducted, Rāma must enter Matañga's Wood, where the ṛṣi Matañga formerly had his hermitage, in order to meet his monkey ally Sugrīva and his monkey companion Hanumān. First, quite surprisingly, given their popularity and prominence in the epic, the *Rāmāyaṇa* seems quite definite in classifying monkeys as inauspicious. When Rāma is about to leave for the forest, his mother Kauśalyā's tearful parting words include this wish: "'May there be no monkeys (*plavagā*), scorpions, gnats, mosquitoes, reptiles, or insects in the deep forest for you'" (*Rām.* 2.22.6). It is clear that the concern is that Rāma's path may be auspicious: Kauśalyā continues to list other animals which she hopes will not harm Rāma, and concludes "'may your arrivals be propitious/auspicious'" (*āgamāste śivāḥ santu*; 22.9). Further, when Sītā, held captive, first sees Rāma's monkey messenger Hanumān, she thinks she must be dreaming and regards the vision of a monkey as an ill omen: "'This I am surely dreaming now, a disfigured (*vikṛtaḥ*) monkey, a vision forbidden by the Śāstras"' (5.30.4ab). Hari Prasad Shastri translates *vikṛtaḥ* here not as "disfigured" but "inauspicious,"[35] which is clearly implied by Sītā's next words: "'May all be well" (*svastyastu*) for Rāma, Lakṣmaṇa, and her father Janaka (5.30.4cd). Sītā also soon adds, contemplating the surprise she feels in finding Hanumān's company pleasant rather than disagreeable: "'Surely having seen a monkey in a dream is not conducive to increase, but my increase is obtained'" (*svapne dṛṣṭvā hi na śakyo 'bhyudayau prāptum prāptaścābhyudayo mama*; 5.33.21). The term here twice translated as "increase" (*adhyudayaḥ*) is certainly within the auspiciousness domain, providing thus further evidence for the consistent inauspiciousness of the appearance of monkeys. It is thus within this context that we should interpret Hanumān's first appearance before Rāma in the disguise of a mendicant (*bhikṣurūpa*; 4.3.3). It would be inauspicious for him to appear as a monkey. Not only that. Hanumān soon turns out to speak perfect (one might say "pure") Sanskrit.

As regards the ṛṣi Matañga, though the *Rāmāyaṇa* does not say this outright, he is well known from other sources as a Caṇḍāla, an outcaste. He has a place in the southern heavenly mansion (*sabhā*) of Yama beside Agastya, Time, and Death.[36] Matañga's associations with impurity are thus multiple. Yet it is in the hermitage of such a ṛṣi, and in the extended surroundings of the hermitage on mount Ṛṣyamūka, that Rāma confronts the domains of purity and auspiciousness in a fashion that reorients him toward his divine mission: the destruction of Rāvaṇa, now required by the latter's abduction of Sītā. This reorientation, a sort of "rebirth" for Rāma, thus holds some parallels to the Pāṇḍavas' sojourn in the "womb of Matsya." As can be seen already, Matañga's hermitage is associated with death. In both epics, one also finds the symbolic encounters with animals: the Pāṇḍavas in the "womb of the fish," Rāma guided by his associations with vultures, monkeys, and the bones of a buffalo demon named Dundubhi. It is here that Rāma makes his pact with Sugrīva to kill Vālin in order to obtain Sugrīva's aid in recovering Sītā. Let us thus look more closely at the sequence of events in Matañga's Wood and hermitage.

When Rāma and Lakṣmaṇa arrive at Matañga's hermitage, they learn that all the ṛṣis there (including Matañga) have passed away. But a mendicant woman named Śabarī remains behind at Matañga's instructions to tell Rāma briefly about the hermitage and its ṛṣis and then, benefitting from Rāma's sight, to ascend to heaven (3.70.19-27). Before he leaves this hermitage to seek out Sugrīva on mount Ṛṣyamūka, Rāma performs ablutions there which he describes as destroying inauspiciousness (*aśubha*) and initiating good fortune (*kalyāṇam*; 3.71.4-5). His visit to this hermitage is thus connected with the turn from inauspiciousness to auspiciousness, but also with an act of purification. All this purity and auspiciousness are most paradoxical, because the place itself is one defiled by a buffalo sacrifice, a specifically non-Vedic and impure rite, that is linked with the story of Matañga's departure from his hermitage and Sugrīva's refuge in its forests.[37]

The good or auspicious turn of fortune which Rāma senses is, of course, his forthcoming meeting with Sugrīva and Hanumān on mount Ṛṣyamūka. There the monkey exiles are protected from Vālin, Sugrīva's brother, by Matañga's curse. Here Vālin had formerly disposed of the impure remains of the buffalo demon Dundubhi. This buffalo asura had challenged Kiṣkindhā, the monkey capital, provoking Vālin's defense. Their fight lasted until Vālin grabbed Dundubhi by the horns and "crushed" (*nispiṣṭa*) him until the blood flowed from his ears. Vālin then hurled off the body: "When it was thus impetuously propelled, drops of blood from the wounds fell out from the buffalo's mouth and were lifted up by the wind toward Matañga's hermitage. Having seen them fall there, the sage, covered with drops of blood, uttered a great curse against the hurler Vālin: 'This [hermitage/wood] here may not be entered by the thrower [of this carcass], for upon entering it he will die'" (4.11.40-42). As I have argued elsewhere, the details of this buffalo slaying, including especially the role of the outcaste ṛṣi Matañga in "handling" the defiling blood of the buffalo's remains, are evocative of ritual details in the sacrificial cult of the water buffalo.[38]

Vālin can thus not harm Sugrīva while the latter remains in Matañga's Wood, on mount Ṛṣyamūka. Therefore, despite the place's associations with impurity, it is auspicious for Rāma as he has been told he will need Sugrīva's help in finding Sītā. Mount Ṛṣyamūka is also where Sītā, seeing the monkeys below, had dropped her auspicious jewels and garment to mark the trail of her abduction by Rāvaṇa. But Sugrīva's aid does not come to Rāma without further indications from Vālmīki as to how these encounters with the ambiguities of purity and auspiciousness affect the hero. It is certainly significant that Rāma should form his "auspicious" pact with Sugrīva in such an "impure" spot. It is a pact involving death, and not only that of the buffalo Dundubhi, but the deaths of Vālin and Rāvaṇa. First, Sugrīva points to Dundubhi's remains, "a great pile of bones that shines like the peak of a mountain," which Rāma disdainfully kicks off to a distance of ten yojanas with his big toe. Rāma does this ostensibly to impress Sugrīva that he is Vālin's superior, but Sugrīva naturally points out that when Vālin killed Dundubhi the buffalo had flesh, making Vālin's feat greater than Rāma's (4.11.46-52). Yet Rāma's dispensing of the bones is also a complementary act to Vālin's hurling of the carcass, and thus one of a number of indications that Rāma and Vālin's careers are to be viewed in parallel. Indeed, Rāma is in many ways Vālin's human counterpart:[39] senior brothers whose throne a junior brother has usurped and/or contested, rightful rulers, descendants of the Sun, conquerors of demons while in exile from their thrones, husbands whose wives are of questionable (at least to some) fidelity. It would thus appear that in killing Vālin, Rāma is killing an animal substitute for himself. If so, this can be related to the situation in the *dīkṣā* where the sacrificer undergoes symbolic death and self-offering preparatory to performing as a sacrificer.[40]

What is most striking in these episodes in the hermitage and wood of Matañga, however, is that though Rāma clearly enters a symbolic realm of death that is thick with themes of impurity, he is never recognizably sullied by it as the Pāṇḍavas and Draupadī are during their year in disguise. The *Vālmīki Rāmāyaṇa* takes considerable pains to maintain Rāma's purity. He never has to meet the caṇḍāla ṛṣi Matañga, who is indispensible to the buffalo-killing scenario.[41] He touches only the bones of this animal, and that only with his big toe! He has numerous dharmic rationalizations for his killing of Vālin. His encounters with such inauspicious animals as vultures and monkeys turn out to be auspicious. But Rāma is clearly unaffected by their potential impurity. A vulture helps him from afar. He does not, like Yudhiṣṭhura, incorporate the name "Heron" (Kaṅka) into a disguised identity,[42] or like all the Pāṇḍavas suffer in an "animal womb." Indeed, Rāma never has to enter Kiṣkindhā, the monkeys' "cave city," whereas the Pāṇḍavas *must* enter the city of king Virāṭa to live "like infants in the womb" taking on impurities as a condition of their rebirth. Yet Rāma does spend the rainy season outside of Kiṣkindhā *in a cave* atop mount Praśravaṇa, awaiting the cessation of the rains and the time suitable for war.

In Rāma's case, then, the accent is clearly on his essential and inviolable purity. He takes on no impurity, like Arjuna. Where it is encountered it is removed with the least possible contact. Yet there is considerable paradoxicality in Rāma's encounters with themes of auspiciousness. There seems to be an assumption that everything which surrounds Rāma must be auspicious, beginning with his wife and his brother Lakṣmaṇa, and even including such proverbially inauspicious creatures as vultures and monkeys. The repetitive lists of auspicious omens that greet Rāma in the forest and in battle are but another example of this intention. In some cases, such as in his forest encounters, it would seem that it is Rāma's purity that renders things around him auspicious; in others, such as with Sītā, it would seem to be his standards of purity that require her to be auspicious. In either case, the *Rāmāyaṇa* seems to treat Rāma's auspicious surroundings as a support system for his purity.

To summarize, one has no trouble identifying instances in the two epics where the domains of purity and auspiciousness have convergent focalizations, but different accentuations. What is pure can be inauspicious, as with Draupadī. What is impure can be auspicious, as with Arjuna. Rāma's purity and Sītā's auspiciousness are sustained throughout the *Rāmāyaṇa*, with only the slightest hints that Rāma might come into contact with the impure, and only the post-war, and possibly "late,"[43] developments concerning Sītā's inauspiciousness. Where the negatives enter the picture in the *Rāmāyaṇa*, however, it is in terms of Rāma remaining pure but aligning himself with "inauspicious" forces, and Sītā remaining auspicious but being suspected of impurity. One sees how differently the two epics treat these matters. The *Rāmāyaṇa* idealizes its figures and presents the negatives only through hints and innuendoes, and in instances which are largely beyond the hero and heroine's control. The *Mahābhārata* confronts the ambiguities directly, and presents a hero and heroine who assume their impure and inauspicious aspects by choice. Thus there can never be any real question of Draupadī or Arjuna's purity or auspiciousness, despite the extremes to which they go in donning opposite garbs.

NOTES

1 I would like to thank Frédérique A. Marglin for her work in clarifying these two domains, and stimulating my research upon their relation to each other in the epics.

2 All *Mahābhārata* citations are of the Poona Critical Edition. All *Rāmāyaṇa* citations are of the Baroda Critical Edition.

3 See Pandurang Vaman Kane, *History of Dharmaśāstra* (*Ancient and Mediaeval Religious and Civil Law in India*), 5 Vols. (Poona: Bhandarkar Oriental Research Institute, 1962-1975), Vol. 4, pp. 267-333; Vol. 5, pp. 366-367, 534-540, 621-622, 719-814 and *passim.* The reference to Varāhamihira, *Yogayātra* 3.14, on dishevelled hair occurs at Vol. 5, p. 622.

4 As Veena Das has pointed out to me (oral communication), *śuddha* refers more to purity of "things" and *śauca* to purification processes, such as concern death and menstruation. This essay was not written with such a distinction clearly in mind. It would seem that it is *śauca* more than *śuddha* notions of purity that apply to Draupadi, but *śuddha* notions that apply more to Sītā. More work is thus needed on this point, and I thank Veena Das for making this clear.

5 R. S. Khare, *Culture and Reality. Essay on the Hindu System of Managing Foods* (Simla: Indian Institute of Advanced Study, 1976), p. 71 and *passim.*

6 See Dan Sperber, *Rethinking Symbolism,* trans. by Alice Morton (Cambridge: Cambridge University Press, 1974), pp. 52-54 and *passim.*

7 See Alf Hiltebeitel, "Draupadī's Garments," *Indo-Iranian Journal* 22 (1980), 98-112; "Draupadī's Hair," *Puruṣārtha* 5 (1981), 179-214; "Śiva, the Goddess, and the Disguises of the Pāṇḍavas and Draupadī," *History of Religions* 20 (1980), 147-174; "Rāma and Gilgamesh: The Sacrifices of the Water Buffalo and the Bull of Heaven," *History of Religions* 19 (1980), 187-223; "Sītā Vibhūṣitā: The Jewels for her Journey," in Oscar Botto, ed., *Festschrift for Ludwik Sternbach, Indologica Taurinensia,* 8-9 (1980-81), pp. 193-200.

8 Hiltebeitel, "Draupadī's Garments"; *idem,* "Draupadī's Hair"; *idem,* "Sītā Vibhūṣitā."

9 One finds both classical as well as diffused ethnological prohibitions on hairbraiding during menstruation; see *Taittirīya Samhitā* 2.5.1, and P. Hershman, "Hair, Sex and Dirt, *Man* 9 (1974), 282-283; cf. Gabriella Eichinger Ferro-Luzzi, "Women's Pollution Periods in Tamilnad (India)," *Anthropos* 69 (1974), p. 128; Deborah Winslow, "Rituals of First Menstruation in Sri Lanka," *Man* 15 (1980), 607-608; see also *idem,* 608-609 on changes of clothes after menstruation.

10 A woman's dishevelled hair is a recognized symbol of inauspiciousness; see above, n. 3 and the Tamil epic *Cilappatikāram* 20, *veṇpā* 2: when the king of Maturai sees the dishevelled heroine he dies.

11 See Winslow, "Rituals of First Menstruation," p. 609: menstruation is "'*sudu veneva,*' becoming white or clean" in colloquial Sinhalese; see also Hershman, "Hair, Sex and Dirt," p. 286; Hiltebeitel, "Draupadī's Hair," p. 203.

12 Thus Bhāravi has Draupadī castigate her husband Arjuna as follows: "My locks hang loose, strewn with the dust of Duḥśāsana's insult; having no one to care for them, and left to

the mercy of fortune, they reproach your valour. Ah, I hope you are still the same Dhanañjaya ('winner of wealth')'' (*duḥśāsanāmarṣarajovikirnair/ebhir vināthair iva bhāgyanāthaiḥ/keśaiḥ kadarthīkṛtavīryasāraḥ/kaccit sa evāsi dhanañjayas tvam*)—as translated and cited in Indira Viswanathan Shetterly (a.k.a. Petersen), ''Reccurrence and Structure in Sanskrit Literary Epic: A Study of Bharavi's *Kirātārjunīya*,'' Doctoral Diss., Harvard University, 1976, p. 187.

13 There are certain reasons to suspect that such themes find their way into the *Mahābhārata* from southern or ''Dravidian'' influences. But the evidence is as yet sketchy. See, however, Hiltebeitel, ''Draupadī's Hair,'' pp. 179-181. Most scholars also regard Bhāravi as coming from the south.

14 See Hiltebeitel, ''Draupadī's Hair,'' pp. 182-183 (nn. 10 and 12).

15 See Hiltebeitel, ''Draupadī's Garments,'' pp. 98-101: I argue that this verse is part of the earliest level of interpolation, earlier than the verses which say that Kṛṣṇa supplied the inexhaustible garments.

16 On women's hairdresser's roles after menstruation, see Winslow, ''Rituals of First Menstruation,'' pp. 609-610.

17 See *idem*, pp. 608-609 on women's white garments and ritual purity.

18 For a suggestive initial discussion of this resonant theme, see Branda E. F. Beck, ''The Goddess and the Demon: A Local South India Festival and Its Wider Context,'' draft of paper to appear in *Puruṣārtha* 5 (1981), in press. By contrast, one will note the rarity of suffering among heroes who represent Viṣṇu and, to a lesser extent, Śiva.

19 This statement applies only to the Vālmīki *Rāmāyaṇa*. The Sītā of the *Mahābhārata's Rāmopākhyāna* is more like Draupadī in these characteristics than she is like Vālmīki's Sītā—a fact which I hope to take up in another article.

20 A style of hair not really a ''braid'' (*veṇī*): the hair is clasped ''singly'' in the back; see Hiltebeitel, ''Draupadī's Hair,'' pp. 184-185; *idem*, ''Sītā Vibhūṣitā,'' 198-199.

21 I limit myself here for the most part to what concerns Arjuna. As far as themes of impurity go, most of what concerns him also concerns his brothers; see Hiltebeitel, ''Disguises,'' pp. 168-174.

22 See *idem*, p. 170.

23 This is indicated nicely by Indira Petersen, ''Recurrence and Structure,'' pp. 318-319 (see n. 11 above) citing *Mahābhārata* references to war as sacrifice and the idea that the warrior is purified by his weapons (14.60.23; 15.44.9).

24 On Arjuna, see Hiltebeitel, *The Ritual of Battle: Krishna in the Mahābhārata* (Ithaca: Cornell University Press, 1976), p. 237, citing e.g. 3.39.1. For Rāma see e.g. *Rām.* 2.21.11.

25 See Hiltebeitel, ''Draupadī's Garments,'' p. 108.

26 I share the suspicion of J. A. B. van Buitenen, trans. and ed., *The Mahābhārata*, Books 2 and 3 (Chicago: University of Chicago Press, 1975), Vol. 2, p. 835: ''while mention is made on occassion of bears (*ṛkṣa*) the classification of monkeys is so predominant that one might wonder whether these 'bears' are not really a kind of monkey.''

27 See Madeleine Biardeau, ''Études de mythologie hindoue (IV), Part II. Bhakti et avatāra,'' *Bulletin de L'École Française d'Extrême Orient* 63 (1976), pp. 207-208; *idem*, ''Études [as above] (V), Part II. Bhakti et avatāra,'' *Bulletin de l'École Française d'Extrême Orient* 65 (1978), pp. 149-157, 187-188 (n. 3). See also Hiltebeitel, ''Disguises,'' p. 149 and *passim*.

28 See not only the *Virāṭaparvan* passages mentioned in Hiltebeitel, ''Disguises,'' p. 149, but also 9.55.30. The latter *Śalyaparvan* passage adds discouragement to the view that the *Virāṭaparvan* is an interpolation; see Hiltebeitel, ''Disguises,'' p. 148, n. 4.

29 See Hiltebeitel, ''Draupadī's Hair,'' p. 194, n. 47.

30 See Hiltebeitel, ''Disguises,'' pp. 149 and especially 161, citing 4.23.23 where Arjuna tells Draupadī that ''she'' (Arjuna the eunuch/transvestite) has ''gone to an animal womb'' (*tiryagyonigatā*) during his/''her'' painful period in disguise.

31 See Hiltebeitel, ''Disguises,'' pp. 154-156 on the ambiguities of Arjuna's sexual identity during his period in disguise.

32 See *idem*, pp. 161-168.

33 On the proverbial impurity of eunuchs, see *Mbh.* 9.30.70-71, and Morris Carstairs, *The Twice-Born: A Study of a Community of High Caste Hindus* (Bloomington: Indiana University Press, 1961), pp. 59-61, 307, 323.

34 See e.g. *Rām.* 6.40.31.

35 Hari Prasad Shastri, trans., *The Rāmāyaṇa of Vālmīki*, 3 vols. (London: Shanti Sadan, 1962-1970), vol. 2, p. 408.

36 See Hiltebeitel, "Rāma and Gilgamesh," p. 204, citing *Mbh.* 2.8.26.

37 For a fuller discussion of what follows, see Hiltebeitel, "Rāma and Gilgamesh," pp. 200-211.

38 See *idem*, pp. 188-211, especially pp. 204-206, 210-211.

39 Of course, so is Sugrīva. The two monkeys are animal doubles not only of conflicting aspects of Rāma, but of Rāma's relations with his own brothers. For this same point viewed from a different angle, see J. Moussaieff Masson, "Fratricide and the Monkeys: Psychoanalytic Observations on an Episode in the *Vālmīkirāmāyaṇam*," *Journal of the American Oriental Society* 95 (1975), pp. 672-678.

40 See Madeleine Biardeau, as cited in n. 26 above, and *idem* and Charles Malamoud, *Le sacrifice dans l'Inde ancienne* (Paris: Presses Universitaires de France, 1976), p. 36.

41 This non-meeting with Mataṅga stands in marked contrast with the important meetings with other ṛṣis earlier in Rāma's forest wanderings.

42 On Yudhiṣṭhira and Kaṅka, see Biardeau, "Études (V)," pp. 99-101 and 104; Hiltebeitel, "Disguises," pp. 169 170.

43 It is frequently argued that the seventh book of the Vālmīki *Rāmāyaṇa* is a late interpolation.

The Two Levels of Auspiciousness in Śrīvaiṣṇava Ritual and Literature

VASUDHA NARAYANAN
University of Florida, Gainesville, U.S.A.

Auspiciousness is of two kinds: one pertaining to this life, the other, to the spiritual way leading to *mokṣa*.

Parāśara Bhaṭṭar—12th Century A.D.[1]

A

THE ŚRĪVAIṢṆAVA *sampradāya* stresses the importance of both theological writings (Tamil: *ācārya vākkukaḷ*) and the traditional way of practising rituals (Tm: *anuṣṭhāṇa muṛai*). A thirteenth century theologian, while working out an elaborate simile, compares the *jñāna* that one gets from scripture and *anuṣṭhāna* to the two wings of a bird; the bird itself symbolised an ideal Śrīvaiṣṇava *ācārya*.[2] Following this rather venerable tradition, I have tried to show some aspects of auspiciousness and purity by the understanding of two rituals in Śrīvaiṣṇava life, alluding to theological discussions where they seem relevant. The two rituals are *Sumaṅgali prārthana* and the sacrament of surrender or *prapatti*. The first ritual illustrates various notions of auspiciousness and purity that are prevalent in everyday life and the second, as they are understood in theological terms.

B

Sumaṅgali prārthana[3] is a ceremonial prayer done by several women whose husbands are living (*sumaṅgalis*, lit. women with *maṅgala*) to a dead *sumaṅgali*, to request *maṅgala*[4] in the family. This ritual is not exclusively Śrīvaiṣṇavaite, it is found in many brahmin sects in South India. *Sumaṅgali prārthana* emphasises auspiciousness (in the use of clothing, jewels, food, symbols distributed, etc.), and is usually done just before the celebration of a major auspicious occasion such as a wedding (Tm: *kalyāṇam*) a sacred thread ceremony (Skt: *upanayanam*), or before entering a new house (Skt: *Gṛhapraveśam*) and is *not* merely euphemistically called 'auspicious'. This prayer is connected with both death and life — the participants include (a) a dead *sumaṅgali* who is invoked by (b) living *sumaṅgalis* led by a chosen *sumaṅgali* and sometimes, (c) a virgin girl of the family; the rituals emphasise auspiciousness in its 'life-promoting' aspects.

The ritual is conducted by any *sumaṅgali*, usually the head of a household. The prayer is addressed to the dead *sumaṅgalis* of the family, who, it is believed, are with God. Basically, the purpose of this ritual is twofold: petitionary and propitiary. (As my grandmother used to explain, one 'celebrates' this ritual to ask for the blessings of the dead *sumaṅgalis* and also to let them know that we remember them.) Neglecting the dead could be "dangerous" for a family for it is quite within their power to bless or curse the living.

On the morning of the prayer, the house is decorated with auspicious symbols: a pennant of fresh mango leaves is hung over the front door and patterns are drawn with a rice flour and water paste on the ground outside the house and on the floors of the rooms where the ceremony is to take place. This is usually the largest room of the house. The *sumaṅgali* who is conducting the ceremony rises before dawn and dips in water all the clothes that the participants will be wearing; the clothes are thus rendered ritually 'pure'. These wet clothes are taken with a long pole and hung in a secluded place; no one is to touch them. The ceremony starts when the clothes are dry.

The *sumaṅgali* now invites four other *sumaṅgalis* formally. These are usually daughters or close relatives of the family and have been fasting since morning (in a manner similar to men who are to perform the *tarpaṇa* or *śrāddha* ceremonies). After an "auspicious" bath (the *sumaṅgalis* are asked to anoint themselves with oil and wash with one of the most visible and common symbols of auspiciousness—turmeric powder) they wear the special clothes that have not been defiled by human touch. They now mark the *Śrīcūrṇam* on their foreheads—a vertical red line denoting the goddess of auspiciousness, Śrī, and a small white half circle at its base, representing the sacred feet of Viṣṇu. The *Sumaṅgalis*' feet are rubbed with *Kum Kum* and turmeric (the ceremony is called *nalaṅgu* in Tamil and only prefaces auspicious ceremonies like weddings) and their hair adorned with flowers. They are supposed to *look* like what they are: auspicious women whose husbands are alive and who are adorned with all that goes with that state.

Fresh decorations are made on the floor; two planks of wood are placed on these and a new *red* sari, nine yards long, that has been specially bought for the occasion and which has also been ritually washed and dried is placed on the planks. Several "auspicious things" (Tm: *Lakṣmī Karamāna cāmānkaḷ*) is kept on the special sari (my mother's list includes the red KumKum powder, collyrium, betel leaves, nuts, pieces of jewelry that are offered for the occasion by the daughters-in-law of the family, and of course the inevitable turmeric powder and flowers. The jewels are later returned to the owners and are considered to be "blessed" by the dead).

On either side of the sari and jewelry are placed two large banana leaves served complete with food. When all the *sumaṅgalis* are gathered, the oldest among them comes forward, lights two silver oil lamps and sprinkles incense powder on some live coals. As a final act, camphor is lit and while the oldest *sumaṅgali* invokes and prays to all the departed *sumaṅgalis* of the family and to God, asking for *māṅgalyam*, all the other participants bow down. Sometimes there is a minor variation: if a young virgin in the family has died, she is included in the prayer, and in honour of her, a sari of shorter length is kept along side the main one. A *kanyā* girl of the family is also included in the ritual and prays along with the other *sumaṅgalis*. Immediately after the ritual prayer, the four participants (and the *kanyā*) are seated in front of the temporary altar and served with food by the *sumaṅgali* conducting the ceremony. After they eat, they are offered betel leaves, flowers and a *dakṣina* (here a monetary gift); the oldest of the four participants is given the special 9 yard sari and the *kanyā* is given the smaller one. They are to wear it immediately; later the saris are folded and hung overnight in a secluded place. Directly below the clothes a jug of water is placed and a lamp is lit: this is for the dead *sumaṅgalis* who are said to return in the night and bless the family and the saris. (The lamp and water sequence echoes the after-death rituals; for the first 13 days, and in some cases, up to 6 months after a person dies, a lamp is lit and water is placed every night in a room where the person died.)

After the gifts (*dakṣina*) are given, the person conducting the ceremony shares the ritual food offered in the two banana leaves to the dead, with daughters-in-law of the family. A word about the menu: in most brahmin families of Tamilnadu, Andhra Pradesh and Karnataka, the food is of the 'auspicious' kind and includes the right lentils, vegetables and spices. The menu usually defines the status of the function; here it is "auspicious"—the kind of food made for weddings and not for death ceremonies. In a ritual which is concerned with remembering the dead, and which associates 'auspiciousness' with it, it is striking that the foods connected with death are avoided.[5]

That night, all the participants of the ritual have a special light meal, preferably just fruits, but most definitely avoiding rice. This again is a procedure followed by men after a *śrāddha* or *tarpaṇa*.

Sumaṅgali prārthana, as the details of the ceremony suggest, involves a "ritual purity" for the participants. This is understood to be strictly of the physical kind, at least by most South Indians today. The Tamil for this is *maṭi*; in Kannada, the word is *maḍi* and the Telugu word is *madugu*. Some of the meanings associated with these words are:

> *maṭi* (Tamil): ceremonial purity, as of one who has bathed; cloth made of the fibre of trees, coarse silk, cotton, etc. as ceremonially pure.
> *maḍi* (Kannada) cleanliness, purity; a washed clean cloth
> *madivalla* - a washerman.
> *madugu* (Telugu) purity; state of being unpolluted; pure or unpolluted cloth.[6]

In popular terminology, this is the isolation or seclusion observed by men and women immediately after their morning baths until they complete their cooking and/or morning prayers. No one is to go near or touch them; they would then be defiled. Several ceremonies connected with death involve this *ācāram*; it is in fact the most widely known aspect of 'purity' in everyday life.

The association of auspiciousness and death in popular ritual is unusual, but not unique. While the time immediately after death is generally believed to throw the family into a state of 'impurity' and 'inauspiciousness' until the thirteenth day[7] when the formal ceremonies of 'adoption of auspiciousness' (*śubha svīharam*) take place, certain kinds of deaths are called 'auspicious deaths' (Tm: *Kalyāṇa cāvu*). This term is used to refer to the death of a person who is reasonably old and has left behind no unmarried children; the dead person is usually a *sumaṅgali* or a man whose wife is already dead. These deaths do not cause a dharmic vacuum in the family. The death of a *sumaṅgali* is perceived to be in the rightness of things, for she has fulfilled her duties and if the husband needs a dharmic partner at all, he always has the right to remarry. The death of an older male member of the family is "auspicious," if his wife is dead. His children are, after all, married, and the dharmic obligations of the family can proceed without interruption. The rituals associated with these deaths are 'celebrated' rather than merely observed. For a *sumaṅgali* the body is anointed with oil, turmeric powder, flowers, etc.; on the day of *śubha svīharam* (13th day after death), saris and other auspicious gifts (betel leaves, turmeric nuts, sandalwood paste, flowers) are given to other *sumaṅgalis*. One is not expected to mourn these deaths for a long time.

Death, then, is associated with auspiciousness in everyday life if it does not interrupt the course of dharmic rituals that are encumbent on a family, or if it is a source of further auspiciousness, as the ritual of *sumaṅgali prārthana* suggests.

Auspiciousness needs to be reiterated; it needs to be invoked and respectfully observed, or else, it will give place to inauspiciousness. One is to propitiate the bearers of auspiciousness; one needs to emphasize its presence ritually. Writing letters or beginning new account books in commercial institutions, one invokes auspiciousness with the writing of the word 'Śrī'; books and scripture end with the words '*Śubham*,' '*maṅgalam*' and musical concerts with the blessing of a song called '*maṅgalam*.' Wealth and flowers are to be respected, for they are the residence of auspiciousness, the residence of the Goddess Śrī. One needs to invite Śrī in the evening to a brightly lit house—the front door is left wide open and the back door is locked. In mythology, Śrī demands this respect; when scorned or ignored, she disappears, taking all the radiance and auspiciousness with her. The disrespect shown to a celestial flower garland by the *Suras*, it is said, causes offence to her (iconographically, Śrī abides in lotuses and flowers) and she disappears. This prefaces the *Kurma avatāra* of Viṣṇu and after much effort Śrī rises from the sea, along with the nectar of immortality *amṛtā*. It is this invoking, this respecting, and an obvious display of practising auspiciousness that we see in *Sumaṅgali prārthana*.

The auspiciousness prayed for is for this life; this is the *preyas* aspect, the *first level of auspiciousness*. One prays for prosperity and happiness, for the longevity of a husband's life, and for death while one has the status of a *sumaṅgali*.

C

The other level of auspiciousness is the theological understanding of the concept—the variety by which one is led on the auspicious path to *mokṣa*. This is seen clearly, I am persuaded, in the *Śrivaiṣṇava* sacrament of taking refuge in Viṣṇu: *prapatti* or *saṁnyāsa.*[8] The ritual of *prapatti* is frequently compared to a wedding. Two of the most important ceremonies of a wedding are the giving away of the bride (*kanyādāna*) and the *māṅgalya dhāraṇa*; the father of the bride gives her to the bridegroom who assumes all responsibility for her well being. The bride's wedded state is now symbolized by "the thread of auspiciousness" (*māṅgalya sūtra*) that she wears: this is the mark which allows her to have the happiness and the "enjoyment" that goes with marriage.

Vedānta Deśika in the thirteenth century A.D. writes:

> The best of preceptors (*ācāryas*) offer their disciples to you (i.e. Viṣṇu) like a father giving away his daughter to a bridegroom. You accept and wed them. Like brides flaunting their "necklaces of auspiciousness" (*maṅgala sūtra*) which allow them to have supreme enjoyment, those humans accepted by you offer loving service to other devotees.[9]

The inner dimension of the sacrament of *prapatti* involves a specific attitude on the part of the participant. He acknowledges his helplessness, his inability to redeem himself from the transgressions and sins of previous lives and with supreme faith (Skt: *mahāviśvasa*) asks Viṣṇu, through the mediating influence of Śrī, to forgive him and grant him *mokṣa.* This can be done only by the grace of Śrī, the consort of Viṣṇu and the ritual itself follows the paradigmatic *prapatti* of Rāmānuja, the most important Śrī Vaiṣṇava preceptor, who in the twelfth century A.D. prefaced his *prapatti* with a surrender to Śrī:

> Having no other refuge, I seek refuge with the goddess Śrī, who is my mother and the mother of the entire world; that Śrī who is the resort of the helpless, who is the consort of the Lord, who is free from blemish...who resides on a lotus, who possesses countless auspicious qualities...[10]

The *prapatti* to Viṣṇu, therefore, is accomplished only by the grace of Śrī; Śrī destroys the *karma* (Tamil: *Viṇai*) of a person and unites him with Viṣṇu.[11] This is the supreme meaning of the word Śrī:

> The word 'Śrī' indicates ... that she is the mediator (*puruṣakara*). She is to be sought as a refuge by all; she seeks refuge with the Lord; she listens to the petitions of the devotee and makes the Lord listen; she takes away the faults of the devotee; through her grace (Tamil: *aruḷ*) she makes wisdom and other qualities rise in the devotee. These are the meanings of the word 'Śrī' denoted by Scripture.[12]

Her auspiciousness is defined in terms of *mokṣa*:

> She is auspicious (*kalyāṇa*) because she gives us the knowledge leading to *mokṣa* and because she is so conformable (*anukula*) to human beings.[13]

As early as the Tamil literature of the Caṅkam period (1st to 3rd century A.D.), Śrī, who is known as Tiru in Tamil, is associated with the ideas of detachment and spiritual advancement:

> ...if this world and *tapas* were weighed in a balance, the [world] is as small as a mustard seed when compared with the latter. If one longs for heaven, one should let go of earthly passion. And so, Tiru will not ever let go those who let go of this world; but she is not attached to those who are attached to [this world].[14]

The importance of detachment from worldly life and attachment to the deity is expressed in the Śrīvaiṣṇava using the words *saṁnyāsa* (renounce, to leave) and *prapatti* (to surrender; to let go) synonymously. The words have a twofold connotation: to let go of attachment to worldly wealth and enjoyment and considering the Lord and Śrī as the source of eternal happiness and fortune. Rāmānuja's cousin Tirukkurukaip pirāṉ Piḷḷāṉ defines the wealth and auspiciousness of the Śrīvaiṣṇava (*śrīvaiṣṇava śrī*) in terms of exclusively 'enjoying' the Lord.[15] This experience (*anubhava*) is considered as *maṅgala*, as auspicious, as the best state (*uttama*) a person can be in.[16]

In literature and ritual, Śrī is associated with the promise of an immortal life: a connection which is reiterated in mythology. Śrī manifests herself with the churning of the ocean and is followed by the nectar of immortality, *amṛta*.

The time of death, then, is a time for rejoicing; one has been led by Śrī on the *Śreyas* path of auspiciousness and physical death signifies that the individual is to enjoy an eternal life with Viṣṇu, a life that was promised by the auspicious (Tm: *Kalyāṇam*) ceremony of *prapatti*. Traditional biographical literature of the Śrīvaiṣṇava community, such as the *Guruparampara prabhavam* ("The glory of the succession of preceptors," circa 13th century A.D.), expresses this view in the narrative sections concerning the death of Parāśara Bhaṭṭar (the preceptor who is quoted at the beginning of this paper) and Rāmānuja. Bhaṭṭar died at a very young age. His mother Āṇṭāḷ is informed of his death and she

> quickly clasped him to her breast. She beheld the glorious wonder (*vismaya*) of her son graciously ascending to the sacred land (*tirunāṭu*). Her heart was not disturbed, her face did not show any grief, she did not cry...she merely said "He who owns the human has taken on the soul that is His property; should we display any displeasure at that?

Āṇṭāḷ later sees her younger son grieving his brother's death and denounces him as not being a worthy child of his father. She rebukes him and asks "Are you envious of the great fortune that is now your brother's? Why do you grieve?"[17]

The *Guruparampara prabhāvam* also says that the funeral rituals of Rāmānuja, the eleventh-century preceptor, included "*sumaṅgalis* carrying auspicious lamps (*maṅgala dīpam*)."[18] This image of auspicious women carrying lamps is projected into the Śrīvaiṣṇava concept of heaven. Rāmānuja's cousin Piḷḷāṉ writes:

> The immortal beings who have unflickering knowledge think that it is their good fortune that [the Śrīvaiṣṇavas] have now come [to heaven]. They wash their sacred feet outside their houses. Like the mother who becomes joyous at the sight of a son who has been separated from her for a long time, [the lord's consorts] are filled with love (*prīti*) at seeing them. With this wonderful love, the Mother (Śrī), the auspicious Goddess of the Earth and Nappiṉai, who have auspicious faces (*tirumukam*) as beautiful as the full moon in the time of rain, come with their divine attendants, bringing with them their supreme wealth which is Śrī Śaṭhakopa, fragrant powders, pots, lamps and other auspicious articles (*maṅgala satkaroparakaraṇaṅkaḷ*) to receive them.[19]

As a ritual leading to the ultimate gift that Śrī can bestow, *prapatti* is intimately connected with auspiciousness. Its intrinsic auspiciousness makes it unnecessary for human beings to select an auspicious time to perform it: it is explained by the 13th century Theologian Periyavāccan Piḷḷai, "The very kind of auspicious time that is specified for those doing auspicious things (Maṇipravala: *maṅgala kāryam*) is obtained by the devotees by chance." He later elucidates: "The day that we begin to believe that the Lord is our protector is the very best day."[20]

The auspiciousness of *prapatti* seems to transcend that of everyday life. Any time is seen fit or auspicious for a person to die:

> While it is said that daytime, the bright half of the month and *uttarāyaṇa* are favourable times to die, there is no rule for one who has done *prapatti* (*prapanna*) ...whether he dies during day or night of man, the *pitṛ* (i.e. the bright or dark halves of the moon), or the *devas* (i.e. *uttarāyaṇa* or *dakṣināyana*), the Lord will take the *prapanna* ... The Lord causes the soul's parting from the body without regard to auspicious times.[21]

Similarly, the importance of dying as a *sumaṅgali* would be minimal for a woman; since everyone is a bride of the Lord through the sacrament of *prapatti*, there is no *prapanna* who would be a non-*sumaṅgali*. Death is seen as uniting the soul with the 'bridegroom,' the *Puruṣa*. Śrī leads the human to Viṣṇu and is therefore considered to be supremely auspicious; but the Lord himself is the source of all good and is also the very essence of auspiciousness.[22]

Prapatti which is known as the 'purest renunciation (*sāttvika tyāga*) does not demand (at least in the theological writings) that ceremonial purity be observed by the participant. Draupadī, it is said, took refuge in Krishna while menstruating, a time in which a woman is considered to be most 'impure'; Vibhīṣana took refuge without as much as a shower after a long journey. While ritual or ceremonial purity is eschewed in Śrīvaiṣṇava writings, the inner dimensions of the word 'purity' are stressed. Aḻakiyamaṇavāḷa Perumāḷ Nayanār (13th century) writes in his commentary on the word 'purity' (Tamil: *tūymai*) in the *Tiruppāvai*:[23]

> Purity: we refer here to the purity of simple *gopis*. When they wash their faces, they do not wash their bodies; when washing their bodies, they do not wash their faces [i.e. their physical purity leaves much to be desired] ... But other than one's relationship with the Lord (*bhagavat saṁbandham*) one does not need any other purity (*śuddhi*); one can be impure. There is no other purity (*śuddhi*) than that derived from contemplation on one's relationship to God. Vibhīsana came without bathing in the sea; Arjuna without bathing, heard the *carama śloka* in the battle field; Draupadī, "without bathing" (i.e. while menstruating), did *prapatti*. Therefore one does not have to search for purity (*śuddhi*) for *prapatti*; one does not have to acquire impurity (*aśuddhi*) either; one is qualified as one is ... purity also means the state of having no other goal [but Viṣṇu].

'Purity' is also a word used to describe the style of life that the *prapanna* is supposed to lead. This is the "stainless" (Skt: *nirmala*, *vimala*) nature of his life; he avoids the company of the wicked, associates with the wise (Vedānta Deśika quotes Kālidāsa, "Even a dull person becomes intelligent by associating with the wise like muddy water becoming pure when treated with lather from soapnut"), offers service to devotees and to Viṣṇu and has "faultless conduct."[24]

Prapatti is also known as *Sāttvika tyāga*, the 'purest' renunciation, because one is taking refuge with Viṣṇu, who is the deity of *Sattva*; as opposed to Brahma who was born of *rajas* and Śiva who was born of *tamas*.[25] Viṣṇu's auspicious form (Skt. *divya maṅgala vigraha*) and Vaikuṇṭha, where he resides, are supposed to be made of *sattva* that transcends *prakriti*. This is the purest Sattva (*Śuddha Sattva*), unmixed with *rajas* or *tamas*. This is the essential difference between Viṣṇu and his devotee: the devotee's *sattva* is mixed with, but dominates the other two *guṇas*. The devotee's purity is relative, the deity's absolute.

The Lord's purity (Skt. *amalatvam*, lit. freedom from defilement) is eternal and continuous. The devotee attains this perfect state of having "the eight attributes" (these include freedom from *pāpa*, old age, death, sorrow, hunger and thirst, accomplishment of all desires, and a will that meets no hindrance) only at *mokṣa*.[26]

D

Sumaṅgali prārthana and *prapatti* are both ritual prayers for auspiciousness—of different kinds. The source of the auspiciousness for *sumaṅgali prārthana* is considered to be the dead *sumaṅgali*; for *prapatti*, the source is, of course, Śrī and ultimately, Viṣṇu. Auspiciousness is only sought from those who possess it: auspiciousness is seen to generate more auspiciousness.

In considering the two rituals and theological discussions on *prapatti* one has to assume two levels of auspiciousness—that of everyday life, and that leading to *mokṣa*: the auspiciousness of a householder (*gṛhastha*) and that of a *saṁnyāsin* are different. In this life, having wealth and a husband are the primary associations of the term 'auspiciousness'; the former obviously leads to a "better" quality of life, the latter holds true because a woman's social status, power, and participation in dharmic rituals depend on her being married, and in some instances, fertile. *Sumaṅgali prārthana* seeks the blessings of the dead for the auspiciousness of everyday life—a life as a *sumaṅgali*, prosperity, and happiness in a new house or success in a new venture. In *prapatti*, the individual renounces such desires and seeks only the supreme auspiciousness that can be given by Śrī: liberation from life.

The imperfections of inauspiciousness and impurity are connected with the realm of the created world, with the realm of *prakṛti*, with what is known in Śrīvaiṣṇava parlance as the '*līla vibhūti*' of Viṣṇu. Auspiciousness, here, the kind that one gets by diligent performance of the *sumaṅgali prārthana*, may improve one's lot and well-being; but it is the auspiciousness of everyday life, the happiness of a *gṛhastha* and is temporary. The other type of auspiciousness transcends this; it seeks to be continuous and eternal. This is the auspiciousness signified by the term '*nitya*' in Viṣṇu's eternally auspicious, eternally pure realm, the '*nitya vibhūti*'. Both varieties of auspiciousness are important in the Śrīvaiṣṇava *sampradāya*; and possibly, I suspect, in other traditions of 'Hinduism' as well.

NOTES AND REFERENCES

1 Parāśara Bhaṭṭar. Commentary on the word '*Śubham*' in the *Viṣṇu Sahasranāma. Bhagavadguṇadarpaṇākhyam*, *Śrī Viṣṇu Sahasranāmabhāṣyam*, ed. Śrī Aṇṇangarācāryar, Kāñci: 1964, p. 10.

2 Aḻakiyamaṇavāḷa Perumāḷ Nayaṉār in *Ācārya Hṛdayam*, ed. and tr. into Tamil by Purusottamanāiṭu, Madras University: 1965.

3 To the best of my knowledge there is no written discussion on the *sumaṅgali prārthana*. The account of *sumaṅgali prārthana* in this paper is based on personal observation and participation in the ritual and also on detailed descriptions of it provided by members of my family and some friends in the last few months. I am especially indebted to my aunt Srimati Pattu Varadarajan (Calgary) and my mother Srimati Hema Rajagopalan.

4 The word 'auspiciousness' has been used as a short-hand term to cover all meanings of the words *kalyāṇa*, and *śubha*. These words are held to be synonymous in the Śrīvaiṣṇava tradition, following Periyavāccāṉ Piḷḷai, a 13th century commentator. Periyavāccāṉ Piḷḷai, commentary on the *Gadya traya*, entitled *katya vyākyānaṅkaḷ*, ed., S. Krishnaswami Ayyankar, Tirucci: 1976, pp. 159 and 236.

The word *kalyāṇam* has come to mean 'wedding' in Śrīvaiṣṇava parlance today.

5 An important exception to this custom is found in the practice of some families of the Tanjavur district. These families cook food similar to the kind made for a *Śrāddha* ceremony.

6 Meanings selected from the Dictionary of Dravidian Languages ed. Burrow and Emeneau, Oxford.

7 A Śrīvaiṣṇava brahmin family is considered to be in a state of pollution until the thirteenth day after death. The number of days varies according to *jāti* in South India.

8 Prapatti is held to be synonymous with *tyāga*, *bharanyāsa śaraṇāgati* and *Saṁnyāsa* by the Vaṭakalai Śrīvaiṣṇavas. The details of the ritual differ between the *Vaṭakalais* and the *teṅkalais*. The former hold *prapatti* (*bharanyāsa* or the transferring of the burden of getting liberation to Viṣṇu) as part of the *Pañcasaṁskāra* rites. The *Pañcasaṁskāra* ("5 sacraments") for Vaṭakalai Śrī Vaiṣṇavas include:

i. *Samasrayaṇa:* the imprinting (branding) of the marks of discus and the conch on the upper arms by the *ācārya*. This can be done at any age.

ii & iii. The giving of a new name (*nāma*) and insignia (*puṇḍra*).

iv & v. The giving of the *mantra* and the rite of *bharanyāsa* or *tyāga*. It is this last sacrament that I discuss in the text.

9 Vedānta Deśika, Śaraṇāgati Dīpika, verse 30 in Śrī *Deśikastotramāla*, ed. Śrī Rāmadeśikācāryar, Oppiliyappan Sanniti: 1970, vol. 1, p. 339.

10 Rāmānuja, Śaraṇāgatigadya, verse 1 in *Śrī Rāmānuja grantha māla*, ed. Śrī Aṇṇangaracāryar, Kāñci: 1974, p. 241.

11 Nammāḻvār, *Tiruvāymoḷi*, 4-8-11.

12 Deśika, Rahasyatrayaculakam, tvayatikāram in *Cillarai Rahasyaṅkaḷ*, ed. Śrī Rāmadeśikācāryar, Oppiliyappan Sanniti: 1972, vol. 1, pp. 235-235.

13 Deśika, Commentary on verse 1 of the *Śaraṇāgatigadya*, ed. Chettaloor V. Srivatsankacharyar, Sri Vedantha Desika Seventeenth Century Trust, Madras: 1968, p. 131.

14 Translated from Puṛanānūṛu, poem 358. *Puranānūṛu*, published by S. Rajam, Madras: 1958, p. 151.

15 Piḷḷāṉ, Āṛāyiṛappaṭi commentary on Nammāḻvār's *Tiruvāymoḷi* 2-7-1 in *Bhagavad Viṣayam*, ed. S. Krishnaswami Ayyankar, Tirucci: 1979, vol. 2.

16 *Ibid.*, p. 505, introduction, by Vaṭakkuttiruvīti Piḷḷai in the *Iṭu* commentary on the *Tiruvāymoḷi*.

17 *Āṛāyiṛappaṭi guruparamparaprabhāvam*, ed. S. Krishnaswami Ayyankar, Tirucci: 1975, pp. 362-363.

18 *Ibid.*, p. 322.

19 Piḷḷāṉ, *op. cit.*, commentary on verse 10-9-10.

20 Periyavāccāṉ Piḷḷai, commentary on verse 1 in *Tiruppāvai mūvāyiṛappaṭi*, ed Śrī Aṇṇangaracāryar, Kāñci: 1970, pp. 7-8.

21 Vedānta Deśika, *Śrimad Rahasya trayasāraḥ*, ed. Śrī Rāmadeśikacāryar, Oppiliyappan Sannidhi, vol. 1, pp. 217-218.

22 This theme is reiterated several times in Śrīvaiṣṇava literature. Śrī is supremely auspicious (*maṅgalam maṅgalānām*) according to Vedānta Deśika (Śrī Stuti, verse 1); Bhaṭṭar, following the Viṣṇu Sahsranāmam refers to the Lord as *maṅgālānām ca maṅgalam* and later says "He extends *maṅgala* to all his devotees" while commenting on name 901. The Lord *is* auspiciousness and so He is called *Svasti* ("well-being", name 903). See Bhaṭṭar, *op. cit.*, pp. 27, 199.

23 The commentary is in manipravala and I have transliterated words of Sanskrit origin in the conventional way, even though they are written in the Tamil script in the edition that I have used. Aḻakiyamaṉavāḷa Perumāḷ Nāyaṉār, commentary on verse 5, in *Tiruppāvai Āṟāyiṟappaṭi*, ed. Śrī Aṇṇangarācāryar, Kāñci: 1970, pp. 43-44.

24 Deśika, *Rahasyatrayasāraḥ*, vol. 1, p. 160.

25 Deśika, *Stotraratnabhāṣyam*, p. 46.

26 Deśika, *Rahasystrayasāraḥ*, vol. 1, p. 232. For a discussion on *amalatvam* of the deity, see John Carman, *The Theology of Rāmānuja*, Yale: 1974, pp. 103-111.

Types of Oppositions in Hindu Culture

FRÉDÉRIQUE APFFEL MARGLIN
Smith College, Northampton, U.S.A.

THIS PAPER OFFERS A CRITIQUE of the kind of exclusive dichotomies that structuralism has made so very current in much of anthropological writings. Lévi-Strauss was inspired by structural phonology. It is from this school of linguistics that he borrowed the idea of binary opposition. The undeniably exciting nature of much of Lévi-Strauss' work has contributed to the widespread use of such dichotomies in anthropological works. I propose to look critically at the exclusiveness of such dichotomies. I do not intend to argue that identifying oppositions does not have an immense heuristic value, but rather that one should not assume *a priori* that oppositions are of the exclusive, distinctive, or privative kind. All these expressions simply mean that the two terms of a dichotomy do not partake of each other; in other words that there is a boundary between the two poles of the dichotomy.

In Indianist studies such types of oppositions have been postulated quite often without the necessary reflectiveness about the possibility that the two terms may not be exclusive of each other. Such exclusivity has more often than not simply been assumed. This is true for example of Dumont's treatment of the pure/impure dichotomy and of Veena Das' treatment of the auspicious/inauspicious dichotomy (see the introduction to this volume). Such treatment may be prompted by the fact that linguistically the terms present themselves at first glance in the form of privative oppositions. In Indian languages this is often conveyed by a privative prefix like *a-* as in the following words: *sauca/asauca*; *pavitra/apavitra*; *śuddha/aśuddha*; *śubha/aśubha*; *maṅgala/amaṅgala*. This linguistic form should not lead us to postulate *a priori* that the terms are opposed in an exclusive or privative manner under all circumstances. In certain contexts and for certain purposes, the opposition may in fact be a privative one but in other contexts the relationship between the opposed terms may be different. This can only be ascertained empirically by looking at the context of use of such expressions.

The sets of oppositions I propose to discuss are those rendered more or less felicitously or appropriately by the English terms pure/impure and auspicious/inauspicious. The choice of these English terms has at least the advantage of being hallowed by usage in the writings of Indianists. I will not in this paper discuss the appropriateness of these English terms, since others in the volume address this question. I will simply focus on the kinds of oppositions that these two antithetical pairs of terms represent. I will argue that neither of these pairs represents an exclusive binary opposition and furthermore that each pair embodies a different type of opposition. That is to say that the way purity relates to impurity and vice versa is different than the way auspiciousness and inauspiciousness relate to each other. Both do indeed express a kind of opposition; the linguistic marker *a-* does express some sort of antinomy or tension between the two terms. But in neither case does it mean that the two terms of the opposition never partake of each other. This is true under some circumstances and untrue under other circumstances. Only through an observation of their context of use can the manner in which the two terms of an opposition relate be ascertained.

Let us first examine the nature of the pure/impure opposition. I would argue that the pure/impure opposition is an asymmetrically privative opposition. By this I mean that the impure has to be kept separate from the pure but that the reverse is not necessarily true; the pure may not always be kept separate from the impure. The asymmetry in the relationship from impure to pure on the one hand and from pure to impure on the other hand was formulated by Tambiah in terms of the direct (*anuloma*, from high to low) and inverse (*pratiloma*, from low to high) order of castes. In his article "From Varṇa to Caste through Mixed Union," Tambiah (1974) argues that the *dharmaśāstra* texts bearing on the generation of new *jati*-s through mixed unions represents a theory of taxonomy in which two principles are at work, namely the hierarchical principle and the key principle. The hierarchical principle corresponds to Mary Douglas' (1966) theory of pollution in which classes are kept separate and bounded; in such a system pollution is whatever threatens the boundaries which keep classes separate, either by crossing them or by being anomalous and thus threatening the classificatory system.

The key principle "proceeds on the reverse principle and generates new classes by mixing or overlapping of prior classes." (Tambiah 1974:192) Tambiah proceeds to substantiate these claims by showing how the rules about mixed unions in the sacred law literature exemplify both taxonomic principles. Basically he shows how unions in the direct order of castes, that is, unions between a man of a superior class with a woman from an inferior class, are permitted and generate new categories, new *jati*-s. This is what is called in the text *anuloma* unions, what anthropologists call "hypergamous" unions.

The hierarchical principle, on the other hand, is exemplified in unions in the reverse order of castes, that is, between men of inferior status and women of superior status. These unions are called *pratiloma* in the texts and "hypogamous" by anthropologists. The products of such unions are outcastes. Thus in the inverse order of castes, Mary Douglas' theory of pollution holds true, the products of the mixing of categories are abhorred.

The asymmetry between the direct order and the reverse order of caste can also be seen in other realms than that of sexual relations. Left-over food given from a superior to an inferior does not produce pollution; the typical example is that of the left-over food from the gods, *praśād*, which is of the same type as the superior patron giving left-over food to inferior servants or the wife eating the left-over food of her husband. Similarly the water in which the feet of a superior person have been washed can be drunk by an inferior person. These phenomena are classified by Tambiah as 'boundary overflows'. These boundary overflows in the direct order of castes are positively valued and correspond to the key type of classification. But boundary overflows in the reverse order of castes are negatively valued and correspond to Douglas' theory of pollution, they are what is at the margin.

Tambiah finds that embodied in the rules about the direct order of castes is a principle of power and dominance of the higher groups over the lower groups. This point has been developed in my paper, "Power, Purity and Pollution" (1977). In that paper I have argued that the key principle can also be found in realms other than that of sexual unions such as occupations and wealth. In those contexts, the relationship between the pure and the impure expresses the privileges which the superior castes enjoy at the expense of the inferior castes.

The asymmetry between the direct and the reverse order of castes corresponds to the fact that movement from pure to impure on the one hand and from impure to pure on the other hand are treated very differently. The pure is not always kept separate from the impure; not in the cases of sexual unions or transfers of food or some other transfers. When the transfers from superior to inferior are closely examined, a principle of dominance and privilege clearly emerges. Wherever the dominion of the superior over the inferior requires it, there can be boundary overflows without creation of pollution. It is precisely Dumont's over-reliance on structuralist notions of binary oppositions which led him to exclude power altogether from the sphere of action regulated by the principle of the pure and the impure.

Dumont's insights apply only in certain circumstances, namely when relationships between castes are in the reverse direction, i.e. from low to high. In the reverse direction, when transfers from inferior to superior are involved, we are faced with an exclusive binary opposition and the principle that the impure and the pure must be kept separate and bounded is upheld. The boundedness and separation of the various groups forming hierarchical society are kept inviolate. In fact violation of boundaries in that order are seen as threatening the basic order of society and as producing chaos. (Cf. Marglin, 1977: 262-263).

Douglas' theory of pollution applies not only at the level of certain types of relationships between the castes, but also at the level of the body. Taking the body as a bounded entity, overflows which cross the boundaries of the body render it impure. It is wellknown that all effluvia from the body are themselves impure and render the body impure. As Veena Das (1982) has pointed out, unbounded or disarticulated states of the body such as flowing hair signify a state of impurity; correspondingly, bounded or articulated states of the body such as bound hair, signify a state of purity. In her summary diagram (see introduction to this volume) Veena Das associates purity with bounded states and articulated states of the body and impurity with unbounded states and disarticulated states of the body. Such a view of the pure/impure dichotomy corresponds to what Tambiah has called the hierarchical principle as well as to Mary Douglas' theory of pollution. In those cases—relationships between castes in the reverse order and states of the body—the pure and the impure form an exclusive binary opposition.

These aspects of the pure/impure dichotomy, however, convey only a partial understanding of these two categories; relationships between castes in the direct order—from high to low—are excluded from such a conceptualization. The pure/impure dichotomy is not in all cases an exclusive binary opposition. In the cases of relationships in the direct order of castes, the opposition is governed by the key principle of taxonomy. In those contexts, the opposition between the pure and the impure is not an exclusive binary one and it signifies a different set of meanings, among which the privilege of the superior castes vis à vis the inferior castes.

In the case of mixings governed by the key principle—for example sexual unions between a man of a superior caste and a woman of an inferior caste—the result is not the creation of a category in which the pure and the impure are found simultaneously, bu the creation of a new class. This new class is pure in relation to inferior classes and impure in relation to superior classes. The key principle generates a multiplicity of categories, all being pure and impure relative to each other. This whole set of meanings is absent both from Dumont's and from Das' understanding of the pure/impure dichotomy.

In order to examine the nature of the auspicious/inauspicious dichotomy, it will be necessary to provide a fair amount of ethnographic information since that opposition has received far less attention than the pure/impure one. When I first analyzed my material on the rituals of the *devadāsī*-s in Puri and realized that auspiciousness and inauspiciousness was a central principle in those rituals, I unthinkingly treated that dichotomy as an exclusive one.[1] In other words events, actions, persons, were either auspicious or inauspicious. It never occurred to me that they could be both and it seems to me now that this blindness came from the fact that in structural thinking dichotomies are taken *a priori* to be exclusive binary oppositions. I became aware of my unthinking assumption about the nature of the opposition between the auspicious and the inauspicious through Professor Vaudeville's reading of my interpretation of the Ratha Jātrā festival. In the reworking of that material that is to follow I would like to record my debt to Professor Vaudeville's insightful comments, and her skepticism about what seemed to her an artificial separation of auspicious and inauspicious events in crucial parts of the ritual.

Rather than try at this point to present the arguments and evidence for the distinctness of the two axes of purity/impurity and auspiciousness/inauspiciousness—arguments which I have made elsewhere (Marglin 1981, 1982)—I will focus on the nature of the auspicious/inauspicious opposition. This will be done through an interpretation of the festival of Naba Kalebara (the festival of the New Body), an enlarged version of the yearly Ratha Jātrā.

Naba Kalebara takes place every twelve years or so, whenever the extra lunar month which is added to the calendar so that the lunar and solar calendars coincide is that of *āṣāḍha*.

A brief description of the festival must precede our discussion. During both the yearly festival of Ratha Jātrā and the festival of the New Body, the main ritual specialists are a group of temple servants called *daitā*s. These temple servants form a group apart in that they are endogamous and do not intermarry with other temple servants. They are non-brahmins who are said to be the descendants of the Śabara tribal chief Viśvabāsu. In the legend of the origin of Jagannātha, it is said that this deity, under the form of Nīḷa Mādhaba, was originally the deity of the Śabara tribals. He was worshipped by the tribal chief Viśvabāsu in the forest in great secrecy. A Hindu king named Indradyumna was instructed in a dream by Viṣṇu to found the cult of Jagannātha (a form of Viṣṇu) with the image of Nīḷa Mādhaba. The king sent his brahmin envoy who after various adventures was eventually able to locate the deity. The image of Nīḷa Mādhaba was made of a bluish stone. When the brahmin was ready to take the image, it vanished. Being again instructed directly by Viṣṇu (in a dream), the king had wooden images built by an old carpenter. This carpenter is said to have been Viṣṇu himself. The carpenter fashioned the four roughly hewn wooden images that are now enshrined in the temple of Jagannātha; these are Jagannātha himself, his sister Subhadrā, his elder brother Baḷabhadra, and the pillar-shaped Sudārśana. The descendants of the tribal chief, the *daitā*s, came to be in charge of the deities at the time of the yearly Ratha Jātrā and at Naba Kalebara.

It must be pointed out that the term Śabara is used in Oriya in two senses: it can either refer to the actual tribe called either *śabara* or *śaora* found in the mountainous region of the southern district of Ganjam or it can refer to tribals in general, the equivalent of the term *adibasi*, 'original dwellers'. The *daitā*s of Puri have no actual connection with tribal peoples of Orissa except in this mythical sense. In fact tribals and untouchables were forbidden entrance into the temple until 1948 when the temple entry act legislation was tested by a group of untouchables and tribals.

The word *daitā* is the Oriya version of the Sanskrit *daitya* meaning 'demon'. The *daitā*s cannot participate in the worship of the deities at any other time of the year and if they were to accidentally touch the deities the temple would become polluted. The *daitā*s are said to be the 'blood relatives' (*rakta samparka*) of Jagannātha. Jagannātha is a sovereign deity who has been viewed by Oriyas, probably since the 13th century, as the real sovereign of their country. The king of Puri is considered to be the living incarnation of Jagannātha. The kings of Orissa were said to rule in the name and by the authority of Jagannātha. Various inscriptions attest to this fact (see Kulke 1978).

The fact of a blood relationship between tribals and a sovereign is known from other sources as well. In the myth of king Pṛthu (see O'Flaherty 1977:123, 324 and Veena Das 1977:72) the birth of this king occurred concurrently with that of tribals. Pṛthu was churned out of the body of the bad king

Vena. In the version given by Veena Das, found in the caste purāṇas of the Modh Baniyas of Gujarat, Pṛthu was churned out of Vena's right hand and the Bhilas (a tribal group) out of Vena's left hand. Thus tribals are viewed as brothers to a king on the left side, so to speak. Such a left-handed association between tribals and kingship will become comprehensible later on.

During the yearly festival of Ratha Jātrā, the deities 'grow old' and are then rejuvenated. At the time of Naba Kalebara the deities 'die' and are 'reborn'. The images of the deities are in the exclusive charge of the *daitā*s for the duration of a fortnight at the time of the yearly festival. During this time, the deities suffer from old age and are rejuvenated. At Naba Kalebara it is the *daitā*s who search in the forests in the vicinity of Puri for the trees from which the new images will be fashioned. When the new logs are brought back to the temple, it is again the *daitā*s who fashion new images out of them and destroy the old images. In other words the *daitā*s are those temple servants who are in charge of the life processes of decay and rejuvenation, birth and death. They are contrasted and opposed to brahmins as well as non-brahmin temple servants who during the rest of the year see to those actions that maintain things as they are, such as feeding, bathing, and dressing the deities; those actions, in other words, which form the content of *pūjā*, the daily worship ritual in the temple.

The festival of Naba Kalebara begins 65 days before the start of the festival in the temple.[2] At that time a group of 20 or so *daitā*s along with some brahmins and two *rājagurus*, representing the king, go on foot to the village of Kakatpur to the northeast of Puri (at some 50 km) where they go to the temple of Goddess Maṅgaḷā. Representatives from the various groups of persons in the party sleep in the temple of the goddess, for it is she who will indicate through dreams where the trees are located. If dreams fail, an elaborate worship of the goddess is then undertaken; she is covered with flowers and the direction and the manner in which the flowers fall from her statue are read as omens giving clues to the whereabouts of the trees. The trees are actually searched only by the *daitā*s, not the brahmins. Large forests of *nīm* trees are found in the vicinity of the temple of Maṅgaḷā. The new images must be made from the wood of the *nīm* tree. When the trees are located, temporary shelters are erected around them, one for the brahmins and another group of shelters for the *daitā*s. The latter group of huts is called 'the settlement of the *śabaras*' (*śabara palli*). The brahmins perform vedic fire sacrifices at the foot of the trees. The trees are then felled and shaped into rough logs. These are taken back on carts to Puri.

The four logs are back in the temple by the time of the beginning of the festival which starts on the last day of the month of Jyeṣṭha. That day is called *snāna purnimā* (the full moon day bathing). The old images are taken in procession out of the inner sanctum carried by the *daitā*s and helped by brahmin temple servants who hold onto silk ropes. The old images are placed on a platform in the northeast corner of the outer compound of the temple alongside the new logs.

The *daitā*s and the brahmin temple servants proceed to drench all the images with water. This water has been collected in 108 pots from the well of the temple of goddess Sitaḷā situated near the northern gate of the outer compound. The water discolors the outer paintings of the old images. After some rituals which we need not go into here,[3] the old images are taken back into the temple on the same day and placed on the floor of the corridor leading to the inner sanctum, in a semi-reclining position, propped up by wooden braces. They are not returned to their usual place in the inner sanctum.

The new logs are carried to the northern part of the outer compound. This area is called Koili Vaikuṇṭha and is the burial ground of the deities. Two temporary structures have been erected at that place. In one of them the logs are placed; there, for the next dark fortnight, the *daitā*s will fashion the 'skeleton' of the new images. No one is allowed to see the proceedings. The noise produced by the axes of the *daitā*s is said to be very inauspicious; anyone hearing them may become blind or deaf or lose their progeny. In order to cover up those sounds, the *devadāsī*s sing auspicious songs outside the structure where the *daitā*s are working, all day, every day. The *devadāsī*s are not allowed inside the structure and must remain outside by the entrance, without being able to see the work of the *daitā*s.

In the other structure the high (vedic) brahmins (who are not temple brahmins) perform vedic fire sacrifices and the rites of "establishment" (*pratiṣṭhā*) of the new images. These are performed on a piece of the new wood. Later on, after the completion of the installation rites, this piece will be cut into four pieces by the *daitā*s and will become the plug which will close a central cavity in the images. This cavity contains the "soul substance" (*brahmapadārtha*) of the deities. In other words, the rites performed by the brahmins and the work performed by the *daitā*s are carried out simultaneously in two separate structures for the duration of one fortnight. Both sets of rites are carried out in utmost secrecy.

At the end of the dark fortnight on the no-moon night, the *daitā*s take the newly carved images into the temple. At that time the *daitā*s are the only ones in the temple. They place the new images next to the old ones. The oldest among them is blindfolded and his hands are wrapped in cloths. He is left alone with both sets of images. All lights are extinguished. In the middle of the night, this man changes the soul substances from the old images into the new ones, in utter darkness and secrecy. It is believed that this man will die within the year. After this awesome deed is accomplished, the other *daitā*s come and take the old images to the burial ground, where the temporary structures were erected, and hack them to pieces. They dig a deep hole and throw the pieces in it. Having accomplished this deed, they all go to a tank in the city to take a bath. This bath inaugurates for them a period of ten days of death impurity. The period of death impurity is observed by their families as well. It is said that since one of their blood relatives has died, they are affected by death impurity. The *devadāsī*s who are the wives of Jagannātha, should on the same kinship grounds also observe a period of death impurity; however, they do not.

During this period of death observances nothing happens in the temple; it is deserted. On the tenth day, the *daitās* take a bath in the same tank and are shaved by the barber. In their houses, their wives break the old pots and replace them with new ones; they also purify the houses with cow-dung. On the thirteenth day, the *daitās* give a feast for certain temple servants; this indicates that the period of death impurity is over. Nothing further happens until the end of the bright fortnight of the intercalary month of *āṣāḍha*.

To recapitulate: during the dark fortnight of that month, the images were fashioned; most of the bright fortnight was taken up by funeral observances and feasting after the tenth and the thirteenth day. Activities resume after the last day of the intercalary month—the day of the full moon.

What then follows corresponds to what happens yearly during the Car Festival. The *daitās*, during the dark fortnight of the regular month of *āṣāḍha*, cover the newly carved images with gum, resin, thread, cloth and chalk to give them their final shape. During that time the door leading to the antechamber of the inner sanctum is closed and no one but the *daitās* can be in the presence of the deities. This period is called *aṇasara*, meaning literally, 'without sap or essence'; in other words 'old age'.[4] Popularly this period is called the period of illness.

During this period the deities are in the sole charge of the *daitās*. Besides the work of renovating the images, the *daitās* carry on the worship of the deities in the "tribal manner," (*śabari pūjā*). They offer the deities only raw food such as fruits, milk, and milk products. I was told that the *daitās*, in tribal fashion, first taste the fruits to ascertain whether they are ripe, and then offer them to the deities. The peels are left on the floor rather than being thrown outside. The *daitās* take up residence near the deities and sleep there unceremoniously. The *daitās* treat the deities as relatives. This sort of treatment is in total contrast to the way the brahmin temple servants worship the deities the rest of the year. Under normal circumstances, such worship by the *daitās* would be considered polluting.

During the fortnight when the deities are in the charge of the *daitās* and are suffering from old age and/or illness, no one is allowed to enter that place. The kitchen lies idle; no food is cooked.[5] It is specifically enjoined that no auspicious sounds should be heard; among other things, this means that the dancing and singing of the *devadāsīs* should be interrupted.

On the morning of the no-moon day, at dawn, the doors are opened and the public is allowed in for what is called 'the viewing of the new youth' (*naba jaubana darśana*). The images are renewed and freshly painted except for the pupil of the eyes. In the case of the yearly Ratha Jātrā, the *daitās* during the period of *aṇasara* remove the outer layers of cloth, resin etc. ... and replace these. At the festival of the New Body, the outer layers and paintings are put on the images for the first time. Later that same day a brahmin temple servant paints the pupils of the images. The next day the images are taken out in procession to the chariots which have been readied for that day and are waiting outside of the temple. The three huge chariots have been specially built for this occasion. Each deity in turn is carried to the chariots, accompanied by a crowd of gong-beaters, fan-, umbrella- and fly-whisk-bearers, all forming a most dramatic pageant. The event is a high point of the festival and is witnessed by hundreds of thousands of pilgrims.

The next significant event of the festival is the performance of the "sweeping of the chariots" by the king of Puri. The king of Puri is heir to the ancient imperial Oriyan dynasty of the "Lords of the Elephants" (*Gajapati*). The king arrives seated in a silver chair carried by several men. He is accompanied by the royal brahmins (*rājagurus*) and his agnates. Alighting from his conveyance, the king ascends onto the platform of the chariots which he sweeps with a goldhandled broom. Having accomplished this most remarkable deed, the king returns to the palace.

The much-awaited moment has arrived for the pilgrims. The huge throng takes a hold of the ropes attached to the chariots. One by one the chariots are pulled by thousands of hands; they journey some two miles down the wide main road to another temple, located to the north-east of the main temple. During this journey—called the "pilgrimage journey" (*tirtha jātrā*)—the deities are on the road, visible and accessible to all, regardless of caste status. Offerings of various kinds fly through the air and crash onto the chariots, thrown by anonymous hands. All the carefully maintained separations, all the rules of purity and pollution, are abolished during the pilgrimage journey of the deities.

By the next day, the chariots have arrived at their destination, the temple of Guṇḍicā. This is a temple with no installed images; it lies empty and dormant for the rest of the year. Guṇḍicā is the name of the wife of the legendary king Indradyumna who founded the cult of Jagannātha. The deities spend seven days in that temple, worshipped by brahmins in the normal manner. After this period the deities are taken back and the same sequence of events takes place in reverse. The deities are returned to their usual place in the inner sanctum by the eleventh day of the bright fortnight of *āṣāḍha.*

I have omitted many incidents and details for the sake of brevity and will invoke some of these as the need arises in the interpretation to follow.

There are basically two sorts of temple servants: those who stand in a kinship relationship to the deities and those who do not. In the former category are the *daitā*s and the *devadāsī*s. The *devadāsī*s as the wives of Jagannātha, are the representatives of Lakṣmī, the wife of the god. They are the auspicious women (*maṅgaḷa nārī*). In the words of one of them: "The inauspicious works (*amaṅgaḷa kāma*) are done by the *daitā*s; whatever auspicious work there is, that falls to us. We do the work of the new Jagannātha, they do the work of the old Jagannātha."

It was in fact this statement that first led me to see the opposition between the *daitā*s and the *devadāsī*s as a structural one. In fact, during the Car festival, the *daitā*s and the *devadāsī*s relate to each other only in an agonistic manner. There are two episodes where the *devadāsī*s sing songs expressing their own and their mistress' (Lakṣmī) anger towards the *daitā*s. In one of these the *devadāsī*s tear the clothes of the *daitā* in charge of the image of Jagannātha. It is also true that during the period of seclusion (*aṇasara*), the *devadāsīs* are specifically enjoined not to perform their auspicious rituals. Furthermore, during the whole of the Car festival, the images of the wives of Jagannātha, Lakṣmī and Bhūdevi—which normally stand on either side of the statue of Jagannātha on the dais in the inner sanctum—are kept in a storeroom. The removal of Lakṣmī and Bhūdevi by brahmin temple servants is the very first action of the festival. The *daitās* are consistently separated from Lakṣmī and Bhūdevi. Such a separation is acted out dramatically in the confrontation between the *daitās* and the *devadāsīs*.

The nature of the auspiciousness of the *devadāsīs*, however, must be qualified, as well as the nature of the inauspiciousness of the *daitās*. Upon the 'death' of the deities, it is the *daitās* who hack to pieces the old images and bury them; the *daitās* then observe a period of death impurity for their blood relatives. The *devadāsīs*, as wives, should on the same grounds be polluted; they, however, do not observe a period of death impurity. They are separated from the inauspiciousness of death. The *devadāsīs* represent the 'wife whose husband is always alive' the *ahya*, the woman who never becomes a widow, the one who is always auspicious. They are the representatives of Lakṣmī and embody sovereignty (see Marglin 1981). The *devadāsīs* are insignia of kingship. They represent wealth, abundance of food, well-being and the active sexuality of the *ahya*—as opposed to the sexually inactive widow.

The *devadāsīs*, however, are not allowed to procreate. They recruit new members to their group through adoption and employ indigenous methods of contraception. Similarly, Lakṣmī is separated from the 'birth' of the deities. Lakṣmī is a goddess worshipped for abundant crops and for wealth but not for children or for health and longevity. Although in the sequence of life-cycle ceremonies, the only life crisis which is classified as being inauspicious is the funeral ceremony, one finds a difference in the degree of auspiciousness of the other life-cycle rites. Even though birth is identified in general as being an auspicious event, it is not as unambiguously auspicious as the wedding ceremony. The *devadāsīs* sing the auspicious songs at the weddings, initiation and temple dedication ceremonies of brahmin temple servants. They do not participate in the ceremonies surrounding birth, although these are also said to be auspicious. The palace equivalents of the *devadāsīs*, called *dei*-s, who sing the auspicious songs at all the auspicious life-cycle ceremonies of the king, are called to sing the auspicious songs at the time of the queen's delivery. The palace women, however, must remain behind a curtain separating the queen's chamber from the rest of the world. This separation of the *dei*-s from the birth chamber parallels remarkably closely the spatial arrangements during the 'birth' of the deities, when the *daitās* fashion the new images. The *daitās* "give birth" to the new images in a temporary structure outside of which the *devadāsīs* sing auspicious songs. The *devadāsīs* are present at the "birth" of the deities, but they are separated from the event which they cannot see.

The types of goddesses who are invoked for the fertility of women as well as for the health of children is typified by goddess Maṅgaḷā. Maṅgaḷā is a goddess quite different from Lakṣmī. First of all she is not a consort, not an *ahya*, for she is represented alone. In songs she is associated with Durgā and has affinities with a goddess such as Sitaḷā. Maṅgaḷā, whose very name means 'the auspicious one', is worshipped on every Tuesday of the month of Caitra (March-April), Tuesday being named "the auspicious day" (*maṅgaḷabāra*). This is the beginning of the hot season and Maṅgaḷā (and other similar goddesses such as Bimalā, Sitaḷā, Śyāmā Kāḷī, Rāmacaṇḍī and Barahī) is worshipped by women for the avoidance of pox diseases. Women make an offering of a milk and cheese drink (called *poṇā*) to the goddess by breaking a pot containing the offering in the middle of the road.[6]

These goddesses are both the senders of disease as well as the removers of disease. They are also associated with female procreation. The double aspect of these goddesses who are associated both with disease and with female fertility has also been noted by Paul Hershman. In his ethnography describing a Punjabi village, such goddesses are generically called *mātā*:

> *Mātā* is a capricious female force, outside the bounds of male control and generally only worshipped by mothers...she is the giver of sons...the sender of smallpox and of disaster. (Hershman 1977:276)

In spite of her name, Maṅgaḷā is not wholly auspicious, nor are the other goddesses similar to Maṅgaḷā who, around Puri, are called by the generic name of *ṭhākurāṇī*. I once questioned a farmer from a village near Puri, asking him what events in his village were considered inauspicious. He replied: "If there is *ṭhākuraṇī*, then you know that inauspiciousness (*amaṅgaḷa*) has come to the village." In this sentence the farmer uses the word *ṭhākurāṇī* to mean a pox disease. To ward the evil away, the goddess is worshipped on Tuesdays by placing earthen jars filled with *poṇā* on the main road of the village, one jar at each entrance to the village. Thus the day of goddess Maṅgaḷā (*maṅgaḷabāra*), is the day when the disease and fertility goddesses are worshipped.

Goddess Maṅgaḷā plays a very important role in the festival of the New Body. It is to her temple that the party in search of the trees first comes and it is she who indicates where the trees are to be found. Given this goddess' association with female fertility, the role of Maṅgaḷā can be linked to the "conception" so to speak of the deities. It is from her that the knowledge of the location of the trees which will become the new images comes from.

When the logs are being fashioned by the *daitās*, the spatial arrangements signify the relationship between the various categories. There are two temporary structures erected. In one of them the *daitās* make the images inside while the *devadāsīs* sing outside, separated from but near the *daitās*. The sound produced by the *daitās* is considered to be very inauspicious; it is neutralized by the auspicious songs of the *devadāsīs*. The birth of the deities is at once auspicious *and* inauspicious. It is significant that the site of the birth of the deities is also the site of their burial.

The high brahmins perform vedic rituals as well as the installation ceremony in the other structure. The two structures represent two dichotomies; that of purity/impurity and that of auspiciousness/inauspiciousness. Part of the brahmins' installation rituals includes the recitation of the *puruṣa sūkta* uttered over the piece of wood which represents the deities. The principle of separation and order is embodied in this recitation which invokes the founding of society from the sacrifice of primeval man.

The *devadāsī*s' presence during the fashioning of the images parallels the role of the palace women during the delivery of the queen. Their presence indicates that the event is an auspicious one but their separation from it signifies that birth is not unambiguously auspicious. There is another ritual when the *devadāsī*s also must remain outside. At the festival of goddess Bimaḷā during the month of *aświna* (September-October; it takes place from the eighth of the dark fortnight to the eighth of the light forthnight of that month) the *devadāsī*s perform their ritual outside of the goddess' temple, by its entrance gate. The temple of Bimaḷā is situated in the inner compound of the main temple to the South West of the temple of Jagannatha. In the songs sung by the *devadāsī*s at that time Bimaḷā is identified with Durgā; she is also associated with Sarbamaṅgaḷā (another name of Maṅgaḷā), meaning "the all auspicious," and other village goddesses. In those songs, the goddess is called "genitrix" (*jananī*), an epithet never given to Lakṣmī in the many songs about that goddess sung by the *devadāsī*s.

The single goddess is present at other focal points of the festival. It will be recalled that the yearly Car Festival is inaugurated by the bathing ritual during which the deities are drenched with water from the well of Sitaḷā. This drenching inaugurates the period of *aṇasara*, a period of illness and of old age. During that time, the *devadāsī*s must interrupt their rituals in the temple. This period, however, is both one of disease and old age as well as one of rejuvenation. It is at the hands of the *daitā*s that the deities are rejuvenated since they emerge young from their period of seclusion. The *daitā*s' work during *aṇasara* is inaugurated by a goddess, Sitaḷā, similar to Maṅgaḷā. Popular exegesis explains the deities' illness as being caused by the drenching with water from Sitaḷā's well. Sitaḷā in this case is both the sender of the disease as well as its remover.

The values of purity and impurity are embodied in the act of painting the pupils on the images. This act is performed by a brahmin temple priest and it takes place after the *daitā*s have left the temple and it has been purified. Painting the pupil of the eyes gives the gift of sight (*druṣṭi*); the latter connotes not only sight but also the power of discrimination, the power of recognizing differences, hence boundaries.

This, however, does not mark the end of the festival. The deities proceed on the road and travel to the temple of a goddess. This goddess, Guṇḍicā, seems to be associated with Durgā. By the side of Indradyumna tank, close to the temple of Guṇḍicā, is a small shrine to Guṇḍicā; there the goddess is represented alongside Śiva with a child Kṛṣṇa taking a thorn out of her foot. This iconography is often found in Puri; it forms the subject of one of the nine small niches around the chariot of Subhadrā, and is named "Durgā of the forest" (*bana durgā*). Such a link between Guṇḍicā and Durgā associates the former with the village goddesses. Such an association is supported by the fact that in Bengal there is a smallpox goddess called Guṭikā *ṭhākurāṇī*.[7] *Guṭi* becomes *guṇḍi* when one moves south from Bengal to Orissa and *kā* become *cā* (personal communication, Ralph Nicholas), thus Guṭikā becomes Guṇḍicā in Oriya. The word *guṇḍi* in Oriya means the same thing as the word *guṭi* in Bengali, namely "pox."

During the deities' seven day visit in Guṇḍicā's temple, they are worshipped by brahmin temple servants in the normal manner. The *devadāsīs* resume their daily rituals and the *daitās* are excluded from the worship. At that time, however, the *devadāsīs* cannot be understood to be the representatives of Lakṣmī; Lakṣmī has been left behind in the storeroom of the temple of Jagannātha. In fact, on the fifth day of the bright fortnight, Lakṣmī comes out of the storeroom. Carried on a palanquin by brahmin temple priests, she goes to Guṇḍicā's temple. She is accompanied by the *devadāsīs* who sing of her anger at being left behind.

The ritual of the *devadāsīs* in Guṇḍicā's temple is unusual; it is the only time that they are separated from Lakṣmī and cannot be considered to be her representatives. Even though the *devadāsīs* perform the same ritual actions in Guṇḍicā's temple as in the usual daily worship of the main temple, Lakṣmī's absence lends their ritual a different meaning. Another minor, but significant, deviation from normal worship is the use of a much greater quantity of sandalwood paste (*candan*) for the ritual of "giving sandalwood paste" (*candan lāgi*).

In Guṇḍicā's temple, the deities are rubbed twice a day with huge quantities of *candan*. *Candan* is a cooling agent also used in the worship of Sitaḷā. When someone is ill, heated by the fever of the goddess, Sitaḷā is cooled by being rubbed with *candan*.

The single goddess reappears at the very end of the festival when the chariots have returned to the temple of Jagannātha, just before the deities are carried back inside. At that time, a *poṇā* offering is made to the Yoginīs. According to local mythology, these female beings are the attendants of both Durgā and Kāḷī. The form of the offering is the same as that offered to the goddesses on the Tuesdays of the month of Caitra. The same milk and cheese drink (called by the same word, *poṇā*) is put in three huge earthen jars. These jars reach up to the lips of the images of the deities, whence the name of the offering: "the lip drink" (*adharāpoṇā*). After the jars full of *poṇā* have been placed on the platform of the chariots in front of the deities, they are broken and their content spills onto the road. The fact that this offering is said to be to the Yoginīs and has the same form as the offering made by women on Tuesdays on the open road, indicates that the deities are at that time associated with what the single goddess(es) stands for, namely disease and health, birth and death.

The single goddess in the form of Maṅgaḷā, Sitaḷā or Guṇḍicā is closely associated with the *daitās*. The function of the *daitās* corresponds to the function of the single goddess: birth and death, illness and recovery, youth and decay. Like the single goddess, the *daitās* are inherently ambivalent beings. I would suggest that the *daitās* correspond to the category of ancestors. Their tribal origins as well as their status of agnatic kin to Jagannātha identifies them with the category of ancestor. Jagannātha's ancestry is to be found in the deity of the tribal Viśvabāsu. The *daitās* as ancestors of Jagannātha must necessarily be agnatic kin.

The similarity between the cult of the ancestors and the cult of the village goddesses has been pointed out by Veena Das; this is what she writes on that subject:

> Ancestors are usually represented by rough unhewn stones, which incidentally also represent deities like Mari (smallpox goddess) and Nata (cobra) ... Among the Coorgs we find that there is an identity in the symbols which represent deities like the cobra deity, the smallpox goddess, and the ancestors. These are not only represented by unhewn stones, but are even placed together in the ancestor shrine or on an earthen platform during the ancestor-propitiation ceremony.
>
> (Das 1977:109, 111)

Goddesses such as Maṅgaḷā, Durgā and Dakṣiṇa Kāḷī are represented by unhewn stones in the villages of Orissa (Eschmann 1978:96). Such goddesses, furthermore, are worshipped with animal sacrifice and liquor. This form of worship is also used by the Coorgs to worship their ancestors. As Veena Das has pointed out, such an ancestor worship was also specified by Gobhila in his manual for domestic rituals (Das 1977:99). She also points out that while the ancestors "have the power to cause great harm, they also have the potential and the interest to bestow wealth and progeny on their descendants." (Ibid:101) In particular she mentions that one of the offerings to the ancestors has to be placed on the bed of the householder, "so that Kāma, the god of love, is pleased."

An association between ancestors and progeny can also be found in the wedding ceremony in Puri today. On the fourth day of the wedding, when the bride and groom are already in the house of the groom's parents, the couple perform their first ancestor worship ceremony (*śrāddha*); the bride prepares the food to be offered. On the same day, the couple perform a ritual for the sake of having a male child called *santāna gopāl* (child Krishna) in which the bride carries in her lap a small boy. The couple engage in their first intercourse that very night. The sequence of ritual actions makes a syntagmatic link between ancestor worship and the obtaining of progeny.

Ancestor worship is the only domestic ceremony which my informants could not classify unhesitatingly as being either *maṅgaḷa* or *amaṅgaḷa*. Some said it was the one, some said it was the other; others told me one thing at one time and another thing at another time; and yet others were of the opinion that *śrāddha* was both auspicious and inauspicious. This information from the kinship domain corresponds to the ritual action at the time of Naba Kalebara and Ratha Jātrā where birth and death, decay and rejuvenation take place simultaneously. If one is not blinded by a literal structuralist mode of thought, it seems clear that birth and death, decay and renewal are so intimately intermeshed as to be one process.

Such a view of birth and death is captured in a Sanskrit saying told to me by one of the *devadāsīs*: "*punarapi janamang, punarapi maranang, punarapi jananī jathare sayanang*" ("again birth, again death, again sleep in the womb of the mother").

But perhaps the most vivid simile for the close interconnection between birth and death is one recorded by Veena Das from an old Punjabi lady who said the following about death: "It is like being shifted from one breast to the other breast of the mother. The child feels lost in that one instant, but not for long." (Das 1979:98) The fact that the 'birth' of the deities takes place in the same location as their burial ground expresses spatially the oneness of the process of birth, growth, maturation, decay, and death.

As far as ancestor propitiation is concerned, my own interpretation of Ratha Jātrā and the role of the *daitās* leads me to understand it as being at once auspicious *and* inauspicious. I would argue that the *daitās* correspond to the category of ancestors. Like ancestors, the *daitās* are associated both with birth *and* death. The myth of the origins of the cult of Jagannātha as well as the myth of the *daitās*' own origins makes the association between the *daitās* and ancestors in a narrative medium. The *daitās*' tribal ancestry links them with Jagannātha's ancestor, the deity of the tribal Viśvabāsu, namely Nīḷa Mādhaba. The *daitās* are the ones who attend simultaneously to the illness and rejuvenation of the deities, as well as to their "birth" and "death." For me the powers of the *daitās* are fertile and ambiguous. Life emerges from death, the latter conceived of as a sleep in the womb. The prohibition on having children which applies to the *devadāsīs* must be understood in terms of the inherently ambiguous nature of birth. The *devadāsīs* unambiguously signify auspiciousness, hence they are separated from birth. This is signified spatially during Naba Kalebara when the *daitās* are fashioning new images in a closed temporary structure and the *devadāsīs* sing auspicious songs outside of it without being allowed to enter or even see the goings-on inside.

I want to emphasize that the coexistence of the auspicious and the inauspicious in ancestor worship, among other phenomena, does not obliterate the opposition by creating a new category. The tension remains between the auspicious and the inauspicious. I would argue that it is precisely this tension, found when the auspicious and the inauspicious coexist, that renders the phenomenon powerful in a certain way. When the *daitās* during the *aṇasara* period of Ratha Jātrā, both attend to the deities' illness as well as rejuvenate them, the coexistence of both auspiciousness and inauspiciousness has a transformative effect of renewal.

The opposition between auspiciousness and inauspiciousness is not an exclusive binary one, but one that lacks a fixed boundary between the two poles. Such a lack of separation or boundary between signs allows them to carry meanings of dynamism such as the flow of time, processes of growth, maturation, and decay, or a dynamic force like *śakti*. The auspicious/inauspicious opposition cannot be rendered graphically as a linear axis with two opposite poles, one positive and the other negative. The auspicious/inauspicious dichotomy is of a different kind than that of the pure and the impure dichotomy. The former opposition fits neither the "hierarchical" principle that generates exclusive binary oppositions nor the "key" principle that generates new classes by mixing prior classes. I would propose to identify the opposition between the auspicious and the inauspicious as exemplifying a "transformative principle." Methodologically, the transformative principle can be thought of as the opposite of the hierarchical principle which generates exclusive binary oppositions. We have thus two oppositions and three principles.

In order to elucidate the properties of the transformative principle, I will illustrate it with an iconography rather than with a diagram. Iconographies can convey richer and subtler meanings than diagrams since they are not only iconic but also symbolic.[8] I propose that the iconography of a snake whose head is joined to its tail captures well the intended meanings. It is especially appropriate since snakes are associated with ancestor worship as well as with a vital force as in the visual representations of *kuṇḍalinī* as a snake. In tantric yoga, *kuṇḍalinī* is visualized as a female snake which represents the energies of the adept. I find such visualization particularly felicitous for several reasons: the joining of the head and the tail corresponds to the fact that the opposites of auspiciousness and inauspiciousness are sometimes found together, just as the head can be found joined to its opposite, the tail. Furthermore, the force which this snake signifies is female, just as the transformative force signified by the opposition of the auspicious and the inauspicious, namely *śakti*, is female. I reproduce here a contemporary iconography from Banaras of Kuṇḍalinī coiled around a *liṅgam*, taken from Rawson (1973):

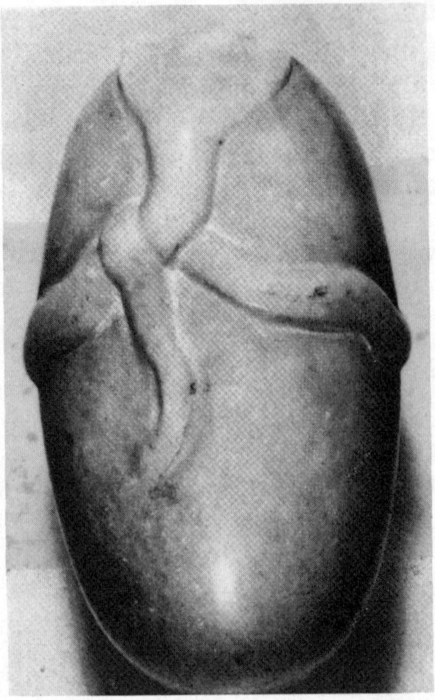

This iconography conveys richer meanings than I have alluded to. I would suggest that this iconography signifies both dynamic and static characteristics. The snake with its tail joined to its head signifies the transformative principle of the auspicious and the inauspicious. When these two opposites are found together, as in the *aṇasara* period of Ratha Jātrā, they signify a potent moment, full of possibilities. The moment is a dangerous one precisely because of its potentiality which can resolve itself in either of the two directions, towards auspiciousness and renewal or towards inauspiciousness and decay. I would suggest that the iconography of *kuṇḍalinī* coiled around a *liṅgam* conveys both the transformative moment as well as its resolution towards the auspicious pole. The resolution is signified by the snake embracing the *liṅgam*. The snake is female and the *liṅgam* is male; the union of the two is the resolution into the stable state of auspiciousness. We find here the same symbolism as that of the auspicious *maithuna*, the couple united in sexual embrace, the auspicious *devadāsī* who signifies kingship, the king being the embodiment of both female and male characteristics and powers (Marglin 1981). The auspiciousness of the *devadāsī*, as everyone told me, also resides in the fact that she can never become a widow; she can never be disunited from her Lord. Female power, *śakti*, signifies the potency of the joining of both auspiciousness and inauspiciousness. In union with a male, the potentiality has resolved itself in a positive direction. This explains why goddesses represented along with their consorts are benevolent, whereas goddesses represented alone are sometimes benevolent and sometimes malevolent. The resolution of the potentiality in a positive or a negative direction seems to depend on a conjunction of happenings; this is where Madan's and Narayanan's findings throw an illuminating light on this issue. The auspiciousness of the events of birth and death depends on particular configurations, be they sociological or astrological.

I would suggest, though, that the union of the male and the female, be it a sexual one or an androgynous one, signifies the stable state of auspiciousness. Birth and death can be either auspicious or inauspicious, since they are both the result of female energy, *śakti*. Their resolution into one or the other pole depends on a conjunction of astrological or other events.

NOTES

1 I wish to express my gratitude to Professor Madan for pointing out to me the inappropriateness of labelling the *daitā*s and the *devadāsī*s "specialists in inauspiciousness" and "specialists in auspiciousness" respectively.

2 For a detailed description of Naba Kalebara see G. C. Tripathi, "Navakalevara: the unique ceremony of the 'birth' and the 'death' of the 'Lord of the World,'" 1978, pp. 233-264. I have supplemented Tripathi's account with descriptions of this festival by my informants.

3 For a fuller description of the rituals of Snāna Purnimā see my forthcoming *Wives of the God-King: the rituals of the devadāsīs of Puri*, ch. 9. (Marglin, 1985).

4 This translation was suggested to me by Professor Charlotte Vaudeville.

5 Khare notes that in the domestic sphere the only time that the kitchen lies idle is at the time of mourning (1976:183).

6 Goddess Maṅgaḷā is also worshipped the whole year, on Tuesdays. If there is no shrine to her, the worship is performed on the open road. See Eschmann 1978:86n.

7 I wish to thank Ralph Nicholas for this reference. The mention of the smallpox goddess is found in an address by J. Z. Holwell, F. R. S., to the President and Members of the College of Physicians in London (A.D. 1767). I reproduce the relevant passage here:

> This disease must then have been of some standing, as those scriptures institute a form of divine worship, with *Poojahs* or offerings, to a female divinity, styled by the common people *Gootee Ka Tagooran* (the goddess of spots), whose aid and patronage are invoked during the continuance of the smallpox season, also in the measles, and every cutaneous eruption that is the smallest degree epidemical.
> (in Dharampal, *Indian Science and Technology in The Eighteenth Century: Some Contemporary European Accounts*, Impex India, Delhi 1971.)

8 I am here using Pierce's trichonomy of signs: index, icon and symbol. In the iconography of the snake coiled around a *liṅgam*, the iconic element is the joining of the two opposites: the head and the tail, as well as the fact that the snake coils around, or embraces, the *liṅgam*. The symbolic element is the femaleness of the snake and the fact that it represents "energy." See Pierce 1932.

WORKS CITED

DAS, Veena

1977 *Structure and Cognition: Aspects of Hindu Caste and Ritual.* Delhi, Bombay, Calcutta, Madras: Oxford University Press.

1979 "Reflections on the Social Construction of Adulthood." In *Identity and Adulthood*, edited by Sudhir Kakar. Delhi, Bombay, Calcutta, Madras: Oxford University Press.

1982 "Epilogue" in the second edition of *Structure and Cognition: Aspects of Hindu Caste and Ritual.* Delhi: Oxford University Press.

DHARAMPAL

1971 *Indian Science and Technology in the Eighteenth Century: Some Contemporary European Accounts.* Delhi: Impex India.

DOUGLAS, Mary

1966 *Purity and Danger.* New York: Praeger.

DUMONT, Louis

1970 *Homo Hierarchicus.* Chicago: University of Chicago Press.

ESCHMANN, Anncharlotte

1978 "Hinduization of tribal deities in Orissa." In *The Cult of Jagannath and the Regional Tradition of Orissa*, edited by A. Eschmann, H. Kulke, and C. G. Tripathi. New Delhi: Manohar.

HERSCHMAN, Paul

1977 "Virgin and Mother." *Symbols and Sentiments: Cross-Cultural Studies in Symbolism.* London, New York, San Francisco: Academic Press.

KHARE, R. S.

1976 *The Hindu Hearth and Home.* New Delhi: Vikas.

KULKE, Hermann

1978 "Jagannatha as the state deity under the Gajapatis of Orissa." In *The Cult of Jagannath and the Regional Tradition of Orissa*, edited by A. Eschmann, H. Kulke, G. C. Tripathi. Delhi: Manohar.

MARGLIN, Frédérique Apffel

1977 "Power, Purity and Pollution: some aspects of the caste system reconsidered." In *Contributions to Indian Sociology*, n.s. Vol. 11, no. 2.

1981 "Kings and Wives: the separation of status and royal power." In *Contributions to Indian Sociology*, ns. Vol. 15, nos. 1 & 2, pp. 155-182.

1982 "Types of sexual unions and their implicit meaning," in *The Divine Consort: Rādhā and the Goddesses of India.* edited by J. Hawley and D. Wulff. Berkeley, CA: Religious Studies Series.

O'FLAHERTY, Wendy Doniger
1977 *The Origins of Evil in Hindu Mythology.* Berkeley and Los Angeles: University of California Press.
PIERCE, Charles Sanders
1932 "Elements of Logic," in *Collected Papers*, vol. 2. Cambridge, Mass: Harvard University Press.
RAWSON, Philip
1973 *The Art of Tantra.* Greenwich, Connecticut: New York Graphic Society Ltd.
TAMBIAH, Stanley
1974 "From varṇa to caste through mixed unions." In *The Character of Kinship*, edited by Jack Goody. Cambridge: Cambridge University Press.
TRIPATHI, G. C.
1978 "Navakalevara: The unique ceremony of the 'birth' and the 'death' of the 'Lord of the World'" in *The Cult of Jagannatha and the Regional Tradition of Orissa*, edited by A. Eschmann, H. Kulke, and G. C. Tripathi. New Delhi: Manohar.

The Pure and the Auspicious in the Jaina Tradition

PADMANABH S. JAINI

University of California, Berkeley, U.S.A.

According to Louis Dumont's well-known thesis concerning the Indian caste structure, the Varṇa system is based upon the fundamental opposition between the respective purity and impurity of the highest Brahman caste and the lowest untouchable, and the relative purity of the two intermediate castes.[1] As valuable as this thesis is for understanding traditional Indian society, however, it is valid only on the presumption that the Brahmans are indeed at the apex of the social structure. His interpretation would not apply to Indian social groups which uphold the major provisions of the Varṇa scheme, while rejecting the traditional hierarchy by degrading the Brahman one step, and similarly upgrading the Kṣatriya, and thus placing the latter at the apex of the social system.

The disjunction between sacredness and temporal power is supposed to account for the superiority of the Brahman and the subordination of the Kṣatriya. While this interpretation is certainly correct within the traditional Vedic varṇa system, when the Kṣatriya is elevated to the highest position, the Brahman can no longer claim superiority on the basis of a purity which he is presumed to embody. The case of the Jainas, who claim to be not only non-Vedic, but even anti-Vedic, in their cosmological view, is of special significance for the study of such social groups as the Śramaṇas.[2]

To illustrate the radical reinterpretation of Dumont's thesis which is necessary when examining such non-Vedic groups, the legend relating the conception of Mahāvīra, the highest spiritual master of the Jainas, is particularly illuminating. We are told that he was originally conceived in the womb of Devānandā, a Brahman woman, the wife of a certain Ṛsabhadatta. However, Indra, king of the gods, who had come to pay his respects to the foetus, became greatly agitated, and the following thought occurred to him:

> It has never happened nor does it happen nor will it happen that arhats, cakravartins ... in the past, present or future should be born in low families, mean families, degraded families, poor families, indigent families, beggar families or Brahman families. For indeed, arhats, cakravartins ... in the past, present and future are born in high families, noble families, royal families, warrior families, families belonging to the race of Ikṣvāku or of Hari or in other such like families of pure descent on both sides. Surely this is an extraordinary event in the world: In the evermoving and endless progressive and regressive time cycles, it is possible that a prodigious exception might occur and an arhat, a cakravartin ... might enter

the womb of a woman from an undeserving clan owing to the potency of the karma pertaining to the formation of their bodies and clans. But they have never been born from the womb of such a woman; they are never thus born, nor will they ever be born. Hence it is the established custom that the embryo of an arhat so conceived is taken from the womb of a woman and is transferred to the womb of a nobly-bred clan. I should therefore have the embryo of the last Tīrthaṅkara transferred from the womb of the Brahman woman Devānandā to that of Triśalā, a Kṣatriya woman of the Kāśyapa gotra, belonging to the Nāṭa clan, living in the Kṣatriya sector (the queen of king Siddhārtha) in the town of Kuṇḍagrāma.[3]

The Jainas believe that Indra ordered his commander of the army, a demigod named Harinegameśi, to conduct the transfer. The scene of the change of embryo (*garbhāpaharaṇa*) is depicted on the Jaina reliefs found at Mathura datable to the first century B.C.,[4] and the event itself constitutes the first of the *kalyāṇakas*, or auspicious events, together with the birth (*janma*), renunciation (*dīkṣā*), enlightenment (*kevalajñāna*) and death (*nirvāṇa*), which are celebrated by the Jainas even today in connection with the career of Mahāvīra.

The most startling feature of the Jaina legend is its strong rejection of the supremacy of the Brahman caste, and its proclamation of the superiority of the Kṣatriya. In the case of Mahāvīra the opportunity to be born as a Brahman was available, and yet rejected. For the other Tīrthaṅkaras as well, the Jainas have ordained that they be conceived only in a Kṣatriya womb;[5] the Jaina position appears to be totally uncompromising in this regard. The Buddhists too maintain that the Kṣatriyas are superior to the Brahmans, but do not prohibit the birth of a Buddha in a Brahman family. A passage in the *Jātaka* states unambiguously: "the Buddhas are not born in a family of Vaiśyas or of Śūdras, but only in the two families of Kṣatriyas and Brahmans."[6] When we compare these two Śramaṇa attitudes, it becomes evident that for the Buddhists, as well as for the Jainas, both the Vaiśyas and Śūdras occupied the same low status as in the Brahmanical system. However, the Buddhist ranking of the Brahman and the Kṣatriya was not fixed. It could be changed according to the will of the people (*lokasammuti*). The Jainas seem to have rejected any such option. For them, the Brahman was forever inferior to the Kṣatriya, although he remained higher than the two lowest castes. The Jaina reasons for maintaining the supremacy of the Kṣatriya must therefore be examined.

One of the reasons for placing the Kṣatriya at the pinnacle of the social order can be traced to the Jaina legend concerning the establishment of human civilization at the beginning of the present aeon (*kalpa*). The Jainas believe that Ṛṣabha, the first Tīrthaṅkara, was the creator of this civilization which began after the Golden Age,[7] when all people were equal and had no rulers. They obtained all of their needs from wish-fulfilling trees and, hence, had no necessity for human institutions of government, or defense, or administration. At the end of this period, however, the magic trees disappeared and new means of survival were required. With the need for food production and the just distribution of resources, the legend says that Ṛṣabha assumed the powers of king and appointed several men as armed defenders (*ugra*) and administrators (*bhoga*). The king as well as these officers assumed the title Kṣatriya. Thus, according to the Jaina mythology, at the beginning of civilization there were only two classes of people, the Kṣatriya and the non-Kṣatriya. Gradually, as Ṛṣabha invented the various occupations of agriculture, animal husbandry, and so forth, the Vaiśya and Śūdra castes (*jāti*) came into existence. There was still no Brahman caste at all.

According to the Jainas, the formation of the Brahman caste is attributed not to Ṛṣabha, but to his son Bharata, the first Universal Monarch or cakravartin of India.[8] It is said that Ṛṣabha ultimately renounced the throne and became the first mendicant of our era, eventually achieving enlightenment and founding the first Jaina monastic order. Under his tutelage, a large number of people assumed the lay vows (*aṇuvratas*), which lead the layman progressively towards greater renunciation of worldly goods and family ties and culminate in the life of a recluse. It is said that Bharata honored these lay disciples with gifts of wealth and marked them with special signs such as the sacred thread, and so forth, by virtue of which they were called *dvija* (twice-born). Their spiritual rebirth apparently released them from the incumbent duties of the other castes. The Ardha-Māgadhī form of the Sanskrit word *brāhmaṇa* is *māhaṇa*. The Jaina texts explain the derivation of this word as *mā hana* (don't kill), which was the advice given by the *dvija*s to Bharata and other kings in conformity with their vows.[9] However ad hoc this etymology may be, it does attest to the Jaina belief that in the secular world there are only three castes and thus no place for Brahmans. Only a person who renounces the world sufficiently to be called a lay disciple may be called a Brahman. This lay disciple has no functions to perform for the material benefit of the society and does not fill any office either at court or the temple; his real associations are more with the ascetic who has totally renounced the world and who comes to be known as the "true" Brahman. The fact that Mahāvīra was not allowed to be born of Brahman parents and yet was given the title *māhaṇa* when he became a mendicant is sufficient to illustrate the Jaina refusal to accommodate the Brahman caste; the secular world consisted of only three castes and was not organized according to divine ordinance such as found in the Vedic *Puruṣasūkta*. While castes eventually became hereditary and may indeed have a hierarchy of their own, this structure lacked any divine sanction and consequently remained entirely secular.

The legend of Mahāvīra's change of womb leads one to question why the Jainas thought it was unworthy of a Tīrthaṅkara to be born into a Brahman family. The story of course presupposes that the Brahman parents were not Jainas, whereas the new parents were followers of Pārśva,[10] the twenty-third Tīrthaṅkara and predecessor of Mahāvīra. But this alone is not sufficient to explain the rejection of the Brahman family. The word *bhikkhāya-kule* (beggar families), immediately preceding the word *māhaṇa*, in the quotation above (p. 84), is very significant: it seems to allude disparagingly to the fact that the Brahmans subsisted on the favors bestowed by others, technically making them beggars. The Jainas have traditionally believed that only a mendicant may beg for his alms; a householder's position is to give, not receive, charity. The

Brahman, by remaining a householder, violates the law when he accepts the gifts given by others, and is thus looked down upon by the Jainas in the same way as they might regard an apostate monk. It should be stated here that, by and large, the Jaina community, as it is constituted now, has no community of Brahmans. The Śvetāmbaras, as well as the Digambaras of the North, do not have a class of priests who perform rituals in their temples, nor do they employ any members of the Hindu Brahman caste to carry out these functions. While they show the incumbent respect to Brahmans, as Hindus would, they do not consider Brahmans superior to themselves. The one exception to this rule is found among Digambaras of Karnataka, who do in fact have a group of priests known as Indra (or Upādhye), sometimes euphemistically known as "Jaina-Brahmans."[11] The Indras are probably Hindu Brahmans converted to Jainism at some time during the early medieval period, who were entrusted with the task of attending to the temple rituals and catering to the needs of the Jaina laity on the occasions of various *saṁskāras*, such as marriage, child-birth, and funerals. Their main source of income is the offerings of food made regularly at the altar by households of a given village and the produce of the land attached to the temples, the proceeds of which they enjoy hereditarily. They are thus comparable to the traditional Brahmans of the traditional Hindu society. There is no intermarriage between the Indras and ordinary Jainas, nor, of course, with the members of the Hindu Brahman community, who treat these Brahmans as non-Hindus.

There is a subtle distinction apparent here which is not without significance for our discussion on purity in Indian society. A Hindu Brahman is considered intrinsically pure and, for that reason, other castes do not hesitate to receive food from him. In the case of the "Jaina Brahman," however, orthodox Jainas who have formally taken the lay vows will not accept food from him even though he may take food from them. The inferiority of the Jaina-Brahman derives not only from the fact that he receives gifts (*dakṣiṇā*) from others for the ritual services performed, but also because he subsists upon the grains and fruits which have been offered by the devotees at the altar of a Jina. These offerings are called *devadravya* (goods intended for the worship of the Lord) and are considered *nirmālya*, fit to be discarded, either by burying them in the ground or by throwing them in water. In traditional Hindu temples such substances would be regarded as *prasāda*, food blessed by the Lord, and thus the purest of substances, which is eagerly consumed by the devotee. For the Jaina devotee, the worship of the Jina is a meditational act, despite its apparent similarity to the Brahmanical *pūjā*. Strictly speaking, there is no deity in the Jaina temple: the Jina, unlike the Brahmanical gods, transcends all pretense of "descending" into an image.[12] The visit to a temple is a meritorious act simply because it reminds the devotee of the Jina's preaching. The Jaina layman regards the temple as the holy assembly (*samavasaraṇa*) of the Jina and imagines the Jina's presence in that image. It would be socially unacceptable to approach such an august assembly empty-handed. The offerings therefore are neither received by the Lord nor blessed by any ritual act on the part of the priest. The "Jaina-Brahman," by eating the offered food, demeans himself and for that reason is considered lower in status than the *śrāvaka*, the initiated Jaina layman. These observations should show that, for a Jaina, neither the image, the offerings, nor the priest are holy or pure. Rather, the idea of renunciation, as symbolized by the image of the Jina,[13] is the source of purity. By extension, only the emancipated soul or his follower, the mendicant, may be regarded as the embodiment of purity. In Jainism, the Śramaṇa replaces the Brahman in the caste hierarchy, leaving no truly defined station for the latter. The Jina or his mendicant disciple may be called a *māhaṇa* metaphorically, but he is certainly not a Brahman in the sense of a member of the classical Brāhmaṇa *varṇa*.

Certain objects of veneration, which are also considered agents of purification are usually associated with the Brahman. One noteworthy example is fire (*agni*) which is thought to be sacred by all Hindus. Being both a divinity (*devàtā*) as well as the priest of the gods, fire is believed to have an innate sacredness of its own. The importance of fire, around which almost all the *saṁskāras* revolve, including those associated with the funeral ceremony, is well documented. Given this pan-Indian belief concerning fire, one would expect the Jainas also to retain some modicum of veneration of fire. But such is not the case if one observes Jaina attitudes both as revealed in their scriptures and in their social customs. The Jainas do indeed include *agni* or fire in their list of astral beings (*jyotiṣka devas*) together with the sun and moon. But *agni* is not considered any more sacred than the other astral beings.

The ancient Jaina texts, on the other hand, repudiating the efficacy of the fire sacrifice, appear to be silent on the role of fire itself. In the post-canonical period, Jainas, especially in the South, undertook the task of integrating themselves into Brahmanical society. It is to Jinasena, a ninth century Digambara *ācārya*, that credit is due for achieving this assimilation at a social level, without compromising the basic Jaina doctrines.[14] He introduced, apparently for the first time, a large number of *saṁskāras* for initiating a Jaina layman into the four-fold *āśrama* scheme, and laid down a variety of ceremonies involving the kindling of the sacred fire and the offering of food in Jaina temples. Explaining the worship of fire, however, Jinasena proclaims:

> Fire has no inherent sacredness and no divinity. But because of its contact with the body of the Tīrthaṅkara [at the time of his cremation], it can be considered pure. Such worship of fire, in the same way that the worship of holy places is made sacred by the Tīrthaṅkara's having attained *nirvāṇa* there, is not in any way blameworthy. For the Jainas, fire is regarded as suitable for worship only on a conventional level. It is in this wise that Jainas worship fire as part of their veneration of the Jinas.[15]

The inauspiciousness of the funeral pyre notwithstanding, the Jainas have thus claimed that whatever sanctity fire has is solely derived from its contact with the dead body of the Jaina ascetic.

What is true of fire is probably true likewise of the other material elements (*mahābhūtas*): earth, water and wind. It is wellknown that the Hindus also regard these elements as sacred and worship them in various forms, considering them to be agents of purity. However, no hymn to earth, such as found in the *Atharvaveda*,[16] is attested to in Jaina texts. Jainas have decried all forms of respect shown to inanimate objects such as fields, stones, mounds or mountains. The Hindu custom of expiatory bathing in rivers and oceans, and worship of the Ganges and other rivers as holy objects, are totally unknown to the Jainas.[17] In fact, the Jainas prefer to use boiled water even for bathing and Jaina monks are not allowed even to touch cold water. All these material substances, including the wind element, are believed by the Jainas to be the bodies of one-sensed (*ekendriya*) beings, who constitute a form of life.

Vegetable life has also been treated by the Jainas in a manner similar to the *mahābhūtas*. The Hindus regard certain leaves, flowers and trees as more sacred than others, and make definite associations between these with certain gods and goddesses. The Jainas, however, have shown a totally different attitude toward vegetable life. The vegetable kingdom for the Jainas constitutes one of the lowest forms of life, called *nigoda*, and they are warned against destroying these beings. The Jainas are forbidden to eat a large number of fruits and vegetables, especially those with many seeds, like figs, or those which grow underground like potatoes. The Jaina spares their lives not because he considers them sacred or inhabited by divinities, but because they are the abodes of an infinite number of souls clustered together. The Jaina mendicant has even stricter dietary restrictions, and is advised to avoid all forms of greens, since they are still alive; hence he subsists mainly on cereals and dried fruits which have no seeds.[18] He may neither kindle a fire nor extinguish one; he may neither draw water from a well nor fan himself. He thus protects the minute life present in these material elements. Even in modern Jaina monastic residences (*upāśraya*) the monks or nuns still live without lights or fans.

These observations should be adequate to show that the Jainas have not regarded as sacred those objects which are universally accepted as pure and auspicious by the Hindus. By repudiating the sanctity of these material objects, as well as of the "sacred cow" and the Brahman caste, the Jainas would seem to have divorced worldly life from the notion of purity. They see sacredness instead in renunciation, which is attributed not to any particular caste but to a group of people: the ascetics who embody renunciation and render other things sacred and pure only by their association with these people.

The Jaina rejection of the inherent purity of the material elements does not imply, however, that the Jainas refuse to accept any object as being auspicious and symbolic of wealth, fame and prosperity. A Tīrthaṅkara's mother, for example, is said to witness certain dreams at the moment of the conception of the child.[19] These dreams include such animals as a white elephant, a white bull and a lion; divinities like the sun, the moon, and the goddess Śrī; and objects like garlands of flowers, vases filled with water, an ocean of milk, a heap of jewels, and a pair of fish. All these are no doubt considered auspicious by the Hindus as well. The Jaina households and their temples are not devoid of some form of these representations. But what is significant is the Jaina insistence that these are not true *maṅgalas* (auspicious objects). They receive such status solely because of local custom (*deśācāra* or *lokācāra*) and, hence, are not sanctioned by the sacred texts.

The Jainas explain the term *maṅgala* as: (1) that which removes (*gālayadi*) impurities (*malāiṃ*); or (2) that which brings (*lādi*) happiness (*maṅgaṃ sokkhaṃ*). The *Pañcāstikāya-Tātparyavṛtti-ṭīkā*[20] enumerates several objects considered auspicious (*maġgala*) by worldly people and seeks to prove that they are *maṅgala* only because of their similarity to particular qualities of the liberated soul. Sesame seeds (*siddhārtha*) are *maṅgala*, for example, only because their name reminds us of the *siddhas* (the perfected beings). A full pitcher (*pūrṇa-kumbha*) is *maṅgala* only because it reminds us of that *arhat* who is endowed with perfect bliss. Similarly a mirror (*mukura*) is to be considered an auspicious object only because it resembles the omniscient cognition of the Jina.

The Jainas are emphatic in their assertion that only ascetics—namely those who follow the Jaina mendicant laws—are truly auspicious (*maṅgala*). These are considered to be four holy objects (*cattāri maṅgalaṃ*)[21] in which a layman takes refuge for his spiritual salvation. They are: (1) the *arhat* or Jina, i.e. one who is worthy of worship; (2) the *siddha*: one who has accomplished his goal, by becoming free from embodiment; (3) the *sādhu*, or Jaina mendicant; and, finally, *dharma*, the sacred law taught by the *kevalin:* i.e. one who is isolated from the karmic bonds. The formula is also called *māṅgalika* and is chanted regularly by the Jaina laity and mendicants together with another sacred formula, the *pañca namaskāra mantra*, or salutations to the five holy beings: namely, the *arhat*, the *siddha*, the *ācārya*, the *upādhyāya* (mendicant teacher), and the *sādhu*. At the end of this ancient formula they finally recite a verse (of unknown date) in which it is asserted that this five-fold salutation which destroys all evils is preeminent (*prathama-maṅgala*) among all auspicious things.[22]

The Indian tradition has unreservedly accepted the holiness of the ascetic, because of his renunciation of worldly possessions. But it is doubtful that he was ever considered to be an auspicious (*śubha*) sight, especially in the context of such festive occasions as the celebration of a marriage, or the beginning of a new business venture. While the ascetic might have represented *śuddha* the purity associated with the transcendental practices which led to *mokṣa*—*maṅgala* was reserved originally only for those worldly, meritorious activities (*puṇya*) which led to the three *puruṣārthas* of dharma, artha, and kāma. The Buddhists and Jainas attempted to assimilate the ascetic ideal into *maṅgala*, not by degrading the *śuddha*, but instead by raising *maṅgala* to a new status which incorporated both the worldly *śubha* and the supramundane *śuddha.*

In this new scheme, anything which was not *śuddha* was considered to be *aśuddha:* activities which were not productive of salvation. However, this *aśuddha* was subsequently subdivided into the mundane pure (*śubha*) and the mundane impure (*aśubha*), i.e., the dichotomies of good and evil, wholesome and unwholesome, which were only conducive to worldly hapiness and unhappiness. Thus, for the Jainas, *maṅgala* came to refer both to the transcendental (*śuddha*), as well as to that portion of the mundane sphere which was pure (*śubha*). A similar pattern seems to be operating in the Theravādin Buddhist division of the meditational heavens into the Suddhāvāsa and Subhakiṇha.[23] The former is "the pure abodes," inhabited by the *anāgāmins* who attain to arhatship from that abode in that very life, whereas the latter is the abode of Brahmās: beings who, however exalted, will return to the cycle of transmigration.

Accordingly, the Jainas begin with the repudiation of the innate sacredness of material objects but allow that an association with the "truly" holy (*maṅgala*) might render them auspicious (*śubha*). The Jaina refusal to allow the integration of the Brahman in their caste system seems consistent with their rejection of a category called "the auspicious" (*maṅgala*) independent of the worldly pure (*śubha*) and the transcendentally pure (*śuddha*).

NOTES

1 Louis Dumont, *Homo Hierarchicus* (Chicago: The University of Chicago Press, 1970).

2 See P. S. Jaini, "Śramaṇas: Their Conflict with Brahmanical Society," in J. W. Elder, ed. *Chapters in Indian Civilization*, I, (Dubuque, Iowa: Kendall Hunt, 1970), pp. 39-81.

3 ...na eyaṃ bhūyaṃ'na eyaṃ bhavvaṃ, na eyaṃ bhavissaṃ, jaṃ ṇaṃ arahaṃtā vā cakkavaṭṭī vā...bhikkhāyakulesu vā māhaṇakulesu vā āyāiṃsu. *Kalpasūtra* #21. See H. Jacobi, tr., *Jaina Sūtras*, Sacred Books of the East, Vol. XXII, pt. 1, p. 225. It should be noted that the Digambara Jainas reject the authenticity of this Śvetāmbara scripture and also do not admit the legend pertaining to Mahāvīra's change of womb.

4 Vincent A. Smith, *The Jain Stūpa and Other Antiquities of Mathura* (1901; reprint ed., Varanasi: Indological Book House, 1969).

5 According to the Jaina tradition all the twenty-four Tīrthaṅkaras of the present age were born into the Kṣatriya families (17 in the Ikṣvākuvaṃśa, 2 in the Harivaṃśa, 1 (Pārśva) in the Ugravaṃśa and 1(Mahāvīra) in the Nāthavaṃśa). For details see Jinendra Varni, *Jainendra-Siddhānta-Kośa*, 4 vols. (Delhi: Bhāratīya Jñānapīṭha, 1970-73).

6 ...Buddhā nāma Vessakule vā Suddakule vā na nibbattanti. lokasammute pana Khattiyakule vā Brāhmaṇakule vā dvīsu yeva kulesu nibbattanti, idāni ca Khattiyakulaṃ lokasammutaṃ, tattha nibbattissāmīti.... *Jātakatthavaṇṇanā*, ed. V. Fausboll, Vol. I, Pali Text Society, (reprint ed., 1963), p. 40. In conformity with this belief the Buddhists have stated that of the twenty-five Buddhas of the present period, twenty-two Buddhas were born into the Kṣatriya families and three (Koṇāgamana, Kakusandha and Kassapa, Nos. 22, 23 and 24) were born into the Brahman families. See *Buddhavaṃsa and Cariyāpiṭaka*, ed. N. A. Jayawickrama, Pali Text Society, 1974.

7 For the Jaina speculations on the origin of the castes, see P. S. Jaini, 1974, "Jina Ṛṣabha as an avatāra of Viṣṇu," in *Bulletin of the school of Oriental anf African Studies*, XL, pt. 2 (University of London, 1974), pp. 321-337.

8 For the Digambara account, see *Ādipurāṇa* (of Jinasena), Part I, ch. 38-40 (Varanasi: Bhārātīya Jñānapīṭha, 1963). For the Śvetāmbara account, see *Triṣaṣṭi-śalākāpuruṣacarita* (of Hemacandra), Vol. I., in *The Lives of Sixty-three Illustrious Persons*, tr. Helen M. Johnson, Vol. I (Baroda: Oriental Institute, 1962).

9 Bharato 'tha samāhūya śrāvakān abhyadhād idam/
gṛhe madīye bhoktavyaṃ yuṣmābhiḥ prativāsaram//
kṛṣyādi na vidhātavyaṃ kintu svādhyāyatatparaiḥ/
apūrvajñānagrahaṇaṃ kurvāṇaiḥ sthyeyam anvayam//
bhuktvā ca me 'ntikagataiḥ paṭhanīyam idaṃ sadā/
jito bhavān vardhate bhīs tasmān mā hana mā hana//
...krameṇa māhanās te tu brāhmaṇā iti viśrutāḥ..../

Triṣaṣṭiśalākāpuruṣacaritra, I, 8, 227-248.

10 On the 23rd Tīrthaṅkara Pārśva, see M. Bloomfield, *The Life and Stories of the Jaina Savior Pārśvanātha* (Baltimore: University of Maryland Press, 1919).

11 For further details on the Jaina priestly castes, see V. A. Sangave, *Jaina Community: A Social Survey* (Bombay: Popular Book Depot, 1959).

12 For a detailed description of the Jaina forms of worship see P. S. Jaini, *The Jaina Path of Purification* (Berkeley: California Press, 1979). It should be noted that many Jaina temples have images of *yakṣas* or "guardian spirits" who are worshipped by the laity. These are invoked by mantras and are believed to manifest themselves in their images. However, the Jaina layman is admonished to refrain from treating them as equal to the Jina and the mendicant is of course barred from even saluting them, since they are inferior to him. See ibid. p. 194, notes 13-14.

13 The reformist Jaina sect known as the Sthānakavāsī rejects even this symbolic representation and regards idol-worship (*mūrtipūjā*) as a form of *mithyātva* (wrong behaviour) even when performed by a layman. See Jaini, 1979, ch. IX.

14 See R. Williams, *Jaina Yoga: A Survey of the Mediaeval Śrāvakācāras* (London: Oxford University Press, 1963).

15 na svato 'gneḥ pavitratvaṃ devatārūpam eva vā/
kintv arhaddivyamūrtījyāsambandhāt pāvano 'nalaḥ//
tataḥ pūjyāġgatām asya matvā 'rcanti dvijottamāḥ/
nirvāṇakṣetrapūjāvat tatpūjā 'to na duṣyati//
vyavahāranayāpekṣa tasyeṣṭā pūjyatā dvijaiḥ/

Adipurāṇa of Jinasena, xl, 88 90

The Buddhist texts go even further and reject all popular beliefs regarding the divinity of fire and water:

sikhiṃ hi devesu vadanti h'eke, āpaṃ milakkhā pana devam āhu/
sabbe va ete vitathaṃ vadanti, aggī na devaññataro na cāpo//
nirindriyaṃ santam asaññakāyaṃ, vessānaraṃ kammakaraṃ pajānaṃ/
paricāriya-m-aggiṃ sugatiṃ kathaṃ vaje, pāpāni kammāni pakubbamāno//

Jātakatthavaṇṇanā, VI, 892-3.

16 *Atharvaveda*, XII, 1 (63 verses).

17 Somadevasūri, a tenth century Jaina author gives a long list of such practices forbidden to a Jaina layman:

sūryārgho grahaṇasnānaṃ saṃkrāntau draviṇavyayaḥ/
sandhyā sevāgnisatkāro gehadehārcano vidhiḥ//
nadīnadasamudreṣu majjanaṃ dharmacetasā/...
varārthaṃ lokayātrārtham uparodhārtham eva vā/
upāsanam amīṣāṃ syāt samyagdarśanahānaye//

Upasakādhyayana, vv. 136-140.
(ed. K. Shastri, Varanasi: Bharatiya Jnanapitha, 1964).

18 No less than thirty-two kinds of plants are forbidden for a Jaina layman. See R. Williams, *Jaina Yoga*, pp. 110-116.

19 For a canonical description of these dreams see H. Jacobi, *The Jaina Sūtras*, Part I, pp. 231-238.

20 For this text as well as for a detailed discussion on the *maṅgala* objects, see Jinendra Varni, *Jainendra-Siddhānta-Kośa*, Vol. III. pp. 251-255.

21 [maṅglasuttāṇi:] cattāri maṅgalaṃ: arahantā maṅgalaṃ, siddhā
maṅgalaṃ, sāhū maṅgalaṃ, kevalipannatto dhammo maṅgalaṃ/
cattāri loguttamā: arahantā ... siddhā...sāhū...dhammo
loguttamo/ cattāri saraṇaṃ pavajjāmi:
arahante...siddhe...sāhū...dhammaṃ saraṇaṃ pavajjāmi//
[pañcanamokkāramaṅgalasuttaṃ:] ṇamo arahantāṇaṃ, ṇamo
siddhāṇaṃ, ṇamo āyariyāṇaṃ, ṇamo uvajjhāyāṇaṃ, ṇamo loe savvasāhūṇaṃ//

Āvassayasuttaṃ, 1-4, Jaina-āgama-series, no. 15
(Bombay: Shrī Mahāvīra Jaina Vidyālaya, 1977).

22 eso pañca-namokkāro savva-pāva-ppanāsano/
maṅgalāṇaṃ ca savvesiṃ paḍhamaṃ havai maṅgalaṃ//

Quoted in R. Williams, *Jaina Yoga*, p. 185.

This is comparable to the refrain "etaṃ maṅgalaṃ uttamaṃ" of the famous *Maṅgalasutta* of the Buddhists. This sutta also lists the perfect virtues of the enlightened person as the best of the maṅgalas:

tapo ca brahmacariyañ ca etaṃ maṅgalaṃ uttamaṃ//

Khuddakapāṭha, p. 3 (Pali Text Society, 1915).

23 For details on these abodes see G. P. Malalasekera, *Dictionary of Pali Proper Names*, Vol. II, Pali Text Society, 1960, pp. 1199 and 1229.

Purity and Auspiciousness at the Edge of the Hindu Context — in Theravāda Buddhist Societies

S. J. TAMBIAH

Harvard University, Cambridge, U.S.A.

Introduction

THE OBJECT OF THIS ESSAY is to suggest that the Theravāda Buddhist tradition, which one may view on the one hand as arising and existing on the edge of the Hindu context, and on the other hand as providing an alternative formulation to Hindu orthodoxy, may by virtue of its very difference help us to appreciate the distinctive structuring of central Hindu conceptions.

Professor John Carman in a preliminary statement he wrote for the workshop held in Washington made the fruitful suggestion that "purity" in the Hindu system is a bifurcate concept: "on the one side there is purity which belongs to material nature—the *sattva* of the three *guṇās* of *prakṛti*—and which is found in greatest measure in the brahman,[1] and on the other side there is another sort of purity separated from the three *guṇās* which is pursued by the renouncer. This latter type of purity perhaps, can be captured in a term such as *paraśuddha.*" I shall try to substantiate that purity in the second sense is central to the path of the Buddhist renouncer.

A second point I shall address is the relation between the brahman officiant and the *bhikkhu* in the Buddhist polities, both in early times in India, and in the later Southeast Asian Buddhist kingdoms, particularly Thailand. In Southeast Asia the brahman and the *bhikkhu*, meeting under the aegis of kingship, were assigned quite different and complementary functions and roles, which might aid us in understanding the relation between "purity" and "auspiciousness" in Hindu India. An instructive contrast to the Buddhist examples is provided by the relation between brahman and king in the Jagannātha cult of Orissa as documented by Professor Frédérique Marglin.

The *Visuddhimagga* ("the path of purification")

An effective way to expound the Buddhist perspective is to document some portions of the *Viśuddhimagga*,[2] the Theravādin classic written around the fifth century A.D. by Buddhaghōsa. It has been called "the principal non-canonical authority of the Theravāda;"[3] besides a summary and interpretation of the basic teachings of the Buddha, it contains a detailed manual for meditation masters.

One thorny problem we have to face in this essay is the translation of Pali (and Sanskrit) Buddhist categories into English equivalents. In the *Viśuddhimagga*, *siddhi* refers to *yogic* powers gained through meditation, and *siddha* to a liberated soul/person. The English index to the text lists "purity" with Pali equivalents as *śuddhi* and *viśuddhi*, but does not list "impurity." It however contains the words "defilement," whose Pali equivalents are *kilesa* and *saṅkilesa*, and "foulness" whose Pali equivalent is *aśubha*.

"Impurity" in doctrinal Buddhism—both in canonical and non-canonical texts—may be said to refer first of all to mental defilements or faults (*kilesa*) such as hate (*doṣa*), greed (*lobha*), ignorance (*avijja*). "Purification" refers to the control or restraint of sensory desires, the closing of the sense doors, and the attainment of a state of detached tranquility. The experience of love (*metta*), compassion (*karuna*) and detachment (*upekkha*) signify this state. In this context of use, "purity" signifies a state of transcendence of and detachment from the phenomenal world; the adept who attains to this condition engages in "detached action": he shows compassion and love for his fellow man without being interested in the fruits of his action. The *arahant* ("saint"), and in particular the *bodhisattva*, are in popular Buddhist thought expected to fulfill these promises.

A second context for the use of the concept of "purity" in Buddhism concerns "the purity of the *sangha*," the Buddhist order of monks divided into monastic communities. One central concern in Buddhism is that the original teachings of the Buddha have been transmitted over time without corruption; the numerous recensions and copying and rewriting of the *Tipitaka* canon is evidence of this preoccupation. A second concern is that the ordination (*upasampada*) of monks has been done in the "correct" prescribed mode and in an unbroken lineage (*parampara*). The alleged re-institutions of correct *upasampada* ordination after a period of decline, and the recurring "purifications of the *sangha*" (*sāsana viśodhana*) recorded in the chronicles, attest to this preoccupation. In fact, both kinds of purifying activities have usually been conducted together at periods of religious revival, which frequently occurred at the founding of new royal dynasties, or after a unification of a kingdom as a result of driving out an invader, or at the time of assumption by an ambitious king of such titles as *cakkavatti* (king of kings) and *dharmarāja*.

Buddhaghosa, the author of *Viśuddhimagga*, cites the passage from a canonical text which opens a window onto the Buddhist renouncer's attitude of mind:

> Now greed (*rāga*) it is, not dust (*rajas*) that we call "dirt" (*reṇu*),
> And "dirt" is just a term in use for greed;
> This greed the wise reject, and they abide
> Keeping the Law of him that has no greed.
> Now hate it is, not dust, that we call "dirt,"
> ....

Delusion, too, not dust, that we call "dirt,"
And "dirt" is just a term used for delusion;
Delusion the wise reject, and they abide,
Keeping the Law of him without delusion.

(*Mahā Niddesa* I. 505).

These verses are typical of the early Buddhist polemics against Brahmanical conceptions—combining irony with etymological play, they caricature and reject the Brahmanical notion of dirt defined "materially" and "ritually" as dust, as body pollution associated with physiological processes of ingestion and excretion, of birth and death, and replace it with a "mentalistic" and ethical notion of defilement as negative emotions of greed, hate and delusion of mind. The dramatic and forceful early Buddhist rejection of Brahmanical ritual notions of purity and pollution is seen in such matters as the open recruitment to the *sangha* from all *varṇas* and castes, the *bhikkhu's* acceptance of cooked food from a lay donor irrespective of his status, and the *bhikkhu's* wilful contamination with death by taking up residence in cremation grounds, using discarded cloth from rubbish heaps, and engaging in contemplation of death as a therapeutic act.

The *Viśuddhimagga* as an overall composition brilliantly demonstrates the Buddhist central tenet that knowledge and wisdom are joined with practice, and that the practice of the meditative exercises provides the experience and understanding of the doctrinal tenets. Knowledge in the abstract cannot be divorced from and secured apart from practice as disciplined conduct.

There is a tripartite ordering to the *Viśuddhimagga.* There is first of all the elucidation of how to systematically cultivate *sīla*, usually translated as 'virtue'; next follows the description of the procedures by which *samādhi*, concentration, is cultivated. Finally, there are the instructions for the cultivation of *prajñā*, insight or understanding. There is not so much a linear as a dynamic relationship between the three objectives.

It has to be understood from the outset that the *Viśuddhimagga's* objective is to show the path that leads to purity (*śuddhi*), and as such it is primarily addressed to *bhikkhus* and not laymen,[4] to seekers who have gone forth from home into homelessness. Purification is to be understood as attaining to *nibbāna* which is "devoid of stains."

Buddhaghosa gives a number of preliminary glosses on what the triad of virtue (*sīla*), concentration (*samādhi*) and understanding (*vipassanā*) signifies. For example, we are told that purification "from the defilement of craving" is the fruit of concentration, and purification "from the defilement of false views" is the fruit of understanding.

Or again, virtue is the avoidance of "devotion to indulgence of self desires," while concentration surmounts sense-desires, and understanding is the means for "surmounting all becoming."

That the three types of activity stand in a hierarchical relation is clearly expressed in their correlation with "the four paths" leading to, or better still, the four stations or levels of achievement terminating in, enlightment: the path of stream entry, the path of once-return, the path of no return and the path of *arahantship*. Here is the correlation: "Likewise the reason for the states of Stream-entry and Once-return is shown by Virtue; that for the state of Non-return, by Concentration; that for Arahantship by Understanding. For the Stream-enterer is called Perfected in the 'kinds of virtue'; and likewise the Once-returner. But the Non-returner is called 'Perfected in concentration.' And the Arahant is called 'Perfected in understanding'" (p. 6).

The practice of virtue implies the "restraint of the faculties," and there are several restraints enumerated such as restraint by the rules of the *sangha* (the *Pātimokkha*), restraint by mindfulness (which guards the eye faculty), restraint by energy by which sense desires when they arise are not allowed to endure, restraint by practising right livelihood and so on. Such "non-transgressions" give meaning to virtue as coolness (*sītala*).

The training precepts for *bhikkhus* are numerous, and expectably the *Viśuddhimagga* discourses with meticulous and forensic eloquence on the propriety expected of the *bhikkhus* (and novices) in their conduct towards one another and towards the public.

The controlled behaviour of the *bhikkhu*, in demeanour, dress, gestures and eating is beautifully discussed in this passage which gives us some sense of the modulated even finicky, majestic even aristocratic, manners inculcated in men who are at the same time ascetic renouncers positively contaminating themselves with the contemplation of decay and the stench of death, and appropriating the rags of the charnel house for their patched-up robes. (Incidentally here lies an important contrast with the matted hair, and long nails, and the ash-encrusted and half-naked body of the stereotype *sannyāsi* of Hinduism.)

"Furthermore, a *bhikkhu* is respectful, deferential, possessed of conscience and shame, wears his inner robe properly, wears his upper robe properly, his manner inspires confidence whether in moving forwards or backwards, looking ahead or aside, bending or stretching, his eyes are downcast, he has [a good] deportment, he guards the doors of his sense faculties, knows the right measure in eating, is devoted to wakefulness, possesses mindfulness and full-awareness, wants little, is contented, is strenuous, is a careful observer of good behaviour, and treats the teachers with great respect. This is called [proper] conduct" (p. 19). The *bhikkhu* is not taken in by externals, neither the "signs" nor the "particulars," he "apprehends only what is really there," such as the ephemeral decaying body that dwells in a woman, laden with jewelry, perfumed and made up, who passes by.

The *Viśuddhimagga* devotes its second chapter to what are called *dhūtanga* which can be translated as "ascetic practices."[5] These practices are conventionally considered today as optional as far as regular *bhikkhus* are concerned. They in fact smack of austerities, and have become the hall-mark in Thailand of wandering monks, dwelling in forests, caves and wild places, who are dedicated to the practice of meditation in seclusion. The Thai expression "*doen thudong*" conveys the sense of walking (and wandering) ascetics.

The meditating monk should undertake the ascetic practices, recommends the *Viśuddhimagga,* "For when his virtue is thus washed clean of stains by the waters of such special qualities as fewness of wishes, contentment, effacement, seclusion, dispersal, energy, and modest needs, it will become quite purified; and his vows will succeed as well" (p. 59).

(1) *The refuse-rag wearer's practice:* the *bhikkhu* collects refuse cloth for robes. *Pamsakula* means "refuse" in the sense of its being found in such a place as a street, charnel ground or midden, or in the sense of its being in a vile state.

(2) *The triple-robe wearer's practice:* the *bhikkhu* has the habit of wearing the triple robe (*ti-cīvara*), namely the cloak of patches, the upper garment, and the inner clothing.

(3) The *alms-foodeater's practice:* the *bhikkhu's* vow is to gather and eat the lumps (*piṇḍa*) of alms food offered by others. (The word *bhikkhu* is derived from *bhikka* meaning alms.)

(4) *The house-to-house seeker's practice:* the *bhikkhu* wanders from house to house collecting food; he is a "gapless wanderer" (*sapadānacārin*) in the sense that he walks from house to house, to all houses, indifferently and without distinction, begging from everyone and showing no preference.

(5) *The one-sessioner's practice:* the *bhikkhu* eats only one meal a day in one uninterrupted session.

(6) *The bowl-food-eater's practice:* the *bhikkhu* receives and eats the alms mixed together in one bowl, and he refuses other vessels.

(7) *The later-food-refuser's practice:* the *bhikkhu* refuses extra food (or further helpings) offered him after his only meal has been concluded.

(8) *The forest dweller's practice:* the *bhikkhu* adops the habit of dwelling in the forest.

(9) *The tree-root dweller's practice:* the *bhikkhu* dwells at the root of a tree.

(10) *The open-air-dweller's practice.*

(11) *The charnel-ground dweller's practice.*

(12) *The any-bed-user's practice:* the *bhikkhu* sleeps on any place that is allotted to him when he is in a community of monks, and in this sense he is an "as-distributed user."

(13) *The sitter's practice:* the *bhikkhu* refuses to lie down, and when resting adopts the sitting posture. (The sitter can get up in any of the three watches of the night and walk up and down, for lying down is the only posture disallowed.)

Vows 8, 9, 10, and 11, relating to the dwelling place of the ascetic, state positively and dramatically the difference between a layman's and an ascetic's mode of life. Of the places appropriate for an ascetic—the forest, tree root, the open air and the charnel ground—it is the forest that best serves as representing the negation of village life. The forest dweller's vow is phrased in one of two ways which illustrates our point: "I refuse an abode in a village," or "I undertake the forest-dweller's practice."

Of the roofless and/or extra-village habitations, the charnel ground is certainly the site that unremittingly and remorselessly brings home to the *bhikkhu* the immediacy of the body's subjection to decay and the illusion of the sense of self as an enduring entity. The cremation ground affords the oportunity to be mindful of death, to vanquish fear and dread, and to observe the very *process* of decaying and of becoming, a true antidote to the fallacies of reification. Thus the *Viśuddhimagga* with its usual attention to concrete details, tells the *bhikkhu* that he should walk up and down the charnel ground looking at the pyre with half an eye, that he should take note of all the objects he sees during the day so that they will not assume frightening shapes for him at night. Moreover, *by no means denying the phenomenal reality of ghosts and spirits*, the manual advises that the ascetic "should not take such foods as sesame flour, pease pudding, fish, meat, milk, oil, sugar, etc., which are liked by non-human beings," and that even if such beings "wander about screeching, he must not hit them with anything."

I have deliberately concentrated on the details of the *dhūtanga* practices because they project in sharp relief the differences between the *bhikkhu's* ascetic regime and the lay householder's mode of life. The ascetic's path is far removed from the layman's preoccupation with auspiciousness and prosperity in a life oriented to the constraints and tasks and values of the phenomenal world. The rule that the ascetic observe no social distinctions between houses as "the gapless wanderer," that he live without a roof over his head as a forest dweller, that he possess the bare minimum of clothes and not amass possessions, tells us not only that he is removed from lay society, but also that he can ensure his neutrality, impartiality and ultimately his universal compassion by avoiding durable relations and reciprocities with laity.

Moreover, the *bhikkhu* strives for a controlled life experience that is different from the layman's life of indulgence: virtue implies the control of his senses, fewness of wishes, and limitations of social intercourse and physical movement. But on the other hand, he also erases the layman's cognitive and affective maps, by crossing the latter's boundaries of social and physical spaces, culinary distinctions, and pure-impure categorisations. The ascetic mixes foods, fusing all tastes, wears discarded clothes, and wanders into the forest. The ascetic, who closes his sense doors while the layman's are open, is also a *breaker* of conventions, a dissolver of man-made cultural categories by which he orders and reifies the world into a durable reality.

Thus it is a necessary corollary of his resolution not to reify that the ascetic is a mindful observer and contemplator of *process*, of growth and decay and dissolution, and what better subject is there for this than the human body and what better viewing ground than a place of cremation?

I would translate these observations into Professor McKim Marriott's "meta-language" for describing Hindu caste transactions thus: the Buddhist ascetic ignores certain rules regarding "mixing" that the layman observes, and at the same time follows his own rules regarding non-mixing and distillation by which he ascends the ladder of spirituality. By virtue of his ability to reach higher, transcending, and encompassing states of consciousness, detachment and wisdom, he has the capacity to "mark" his disciples and lay followers and thus to transfer to them a part of his virtue.

The Buddhist (and Jaina) formulations appear to keep quite separate notions of purity from notions of auspiciousness. In the Buddhist "cosmology," purification has to do with the ascetic's *upward* path of transcending the grosser states of sense and form and materiality, and the mental states of greed, anger and delusion. Purification is that path of life-and-world transcendence.

Auspiciousness has to do with the *downward* path of world formation and differentiation from an initial state of spiritual essence. Auspiciousness is life-affirming and is concerned with providing the favourable conditions for prosperity, wealth, and good health.

These are quite separate and "opposed" cosmological paths and processes, and I shall describe how in the historical Southeast Asian Buddhist societies, this demarcation was implemented.[6]

Brahman, bhikkhu, and king in Theravāda societies

Both in the Buddhist polities of early India,[7] and in those of Southeast Asia, the *bhikkhu* and the brahman co-existed as functionaries. There were however assigned quite different "functions" and fields of action. Their coexistence was achieved under the aegis and patronage of the king. In all Buddhist Southeast Asian kingdoms, Brahmans were employed as court functionaries. They did not comprise a caste or status order within the larger society, they were foreign imports who were gradually "indigenised," and their place in the society was owed principally to their employment by the royal court and its satellite lesser rulers and chiefs.[8] If in India, especially since early medieval times, the brahman and the *bhikkhu* developed an antagonism which came to a climax at the time of Shankara's revivalism, in Southeast Asia they settled into a complementary and non-competitive relationship.

The division of labour between them was roughly as follows. The Brahmans were scribes and *pandits* who codified and interpreted legal codes; they were court astrologers who set the ritual calendar and read the signs; most important of all they performed the *maṅgala* auspicious and prosperity-inducing royal cosmic rites: life-cycle rites like topknot cutting, the *abhiṣeka* consecration of kings, the first ploughing, rites dedicated to the palladium of the kingdom (like the Emerald Buddha), and so on.

Characteristically, the *bhikkhu* did not officiate at these *maṅgala* rites and festivities, for the normative definition was that the *bhikkhu's* vocation was directed to achieving liberation. The *sangha* dedicated to this higher path had to be both protected and materially provided for by the king, the foremost of the householders, and the laity. The ideology of merit-making has it that the *sangha* exists as a "merit field" (*punnak khetta*) in which the laity plough and sow and reap merit. Thus the king as the ordinator of society, as the *dharmarāja*, backed by his people, provides the material and social context and conditions, so that the *sangha* can practice its discipline (*vinaya*) and seek salvation.

In actual fact the Buddhist monks were usually present at the court ceremonies of the Ayuthayan and Bangkok dynasties not so much as the officiating priests (the role of the Brahmans) but as "witnesses" who were worthy recipients of donations and gifts, and as chanters of the *paritta* chants of "protection" which recalled the victories and virtues of the Buddha.[9] A remarkable example of the differentiated participation of brahman and *bhikkhu* is provided by the New Palace Inscription of A.D. 1102 which describes the rituals performed at various stages of the building of King Kyanzittha's palace in Pagan.[10] The main Buddhist ceremonies took place immediately after the first ceremonial act of making offerings to Indra, the *devas*, and all the images of Buddha in the city of Pagan. The Buddhist monks, especially the *sangha* dignitaries, recited the *paritta* verses and sprinkled lustral water at various points of the palace site and over the posts and the places where holes for planting them were to be dug. After this ceremony of "protection," the monks had no other role to play in the actual building operations. All the auspicious rituals associated with the palace construction were conducted by the brahman functionaries and palace officials—such as the initiation of the digging of holes by pressing into the ground a gold peg with seven silver cords attached, the thread used being "spun by virgin daughters of Brahmans"; and the planting of the posts of the throne room, their bases wound with white cloth and the holes having first been fed with boiled rice, fresh milk, and the five kinds of gems, while the king looked on, seated on his elephant.

So far we have focused on the demarcation between the ascetic path of "purification" and the *maṅgala*-conferring activities of auspicious ritual, the first assigned to the *bhikkhu*, the second to the brahman officiant, as it found expression under the aegis of kingship. But this demarcation was not in the kingdoms of Burma, Thailand, Laos and Cambodia only confined to the palace and court, although that was the prestigious centre from which such rites and the conceptions they embodied were radially propagated to the society at large. This process of diffusion by which "The King's state is reproduced in miniature by his vassals" has been illuminated by Hocart.[11] I have documented elsewhere a similar division of labour in Thai village rituals.[12] The *bhikkhu* is chiefly (but not exclusively) engaged in collective merit-making rites, and most importantly, presides over the mortuary rites; he receives gifts, transfers merit, and mediates between life and death/rebirth. There is another village officiant who is called *paahm*, etymologically derived from brahman, or *maukhwan*, who performs the *monghkhon* (*maṅgala*) rites of recalling the *khwan* or spirit essence. The *khwan* rites are primarily concerned with initiation into new statuses at birth, marriage, ordination, with various threshold situations in the life of individuals, and with the activities of households bearing on their prosperity, their recruitment of new members, and their establishment.

While the village monks are typically unmarried youth, at the threshold of adulthood, who undergo the ascetic discipline for a brief period before returning to lay life and marrying and setting up a new household, the *paahm/mau khwan* is typically a village elder, householder, ex-monk, who acquired his literacy while residing in the monastery.

There is no contradiction between the monk's ritual and the *khwan* rites. In fact in the Thai village context there is a direct reciprocity between elders as *paahm* and their children or grandchildren (*luug-laan*) on the one side, and on the other, between monks (as *luug-laan*) and elders to whom merit is transferred. A number of reciprocal oppositions hang together and may be summarised as follows:

Gift giving	Asceticism
Paahm/householder	Monk
(Normal) Secular life	(Abnormal) Sacred life
Elders (*phuu thaw*)	Male youth (*luug-laan*)

The Orissa Jagannātha Cult: Brahman and King in a Hindu Context

The dramatic difference between the relation between brahman officiant and king in a Buddhist polity like Thailand, and in a Hindu polity in India, can be seen if we compare the Thai court ritual with say the Jagannātha cult of Orissa. Professor Frédérique Marglin's study provides us with pertinent evidence.[13]

The king's relation to the deity Viṣṇu (i.e. Jagannātha) is that on the one hand he is a partial or incomplete incarnation of the deity and on the other hand he is the deity's "first servant," in which capacity he acts as "the sweeper" of the deity's chariot. There is an analogy between the God as the "unmovable" transcendent deity, and the king as the "movable" realised deity taken out in processions (*acalanti viṣṇu/calanti viṣṇu*). The issue of the relation between king and brahman must take into account the division of brahmans into different status groups or categories. The distinction between the *śāsan* brahmans and the brahmans who are "temple servants" is an important one, and it is the king's relation to the former that dramatically differs from the Thai case.

The *śāsan* brahmans do not "serve" the deity as *sebākas*; they perform the high *abhiṣeka* ceremonies of consecration of Jagannātha in the temple, and the *abhiṣeka* installation of the king. The *rājaguru* is selected from their ranks. They are receivers of royal land grants (*inām*), and representatives from the *śāsan* villages constitute the *mukti maṇḍapa*, which is a platform in the south side of the inner courtyard of the temple, and also referred to as the seat of Brahma who is the source of the Vedas, of all laws and knowledge of the universe, and who as the ground of all things is not directly worshipped. The platform is said to be located at the exact spot at which the *pratiṣthā* foundation ceremony for the building of the temple was held, thus linking the temple's consecration with the assembly of *śāsan* brahmans.

While the king is never worshipped by the *śāsan* brahmans, there are occasions when the king worships them. At the royal *abhiṣeka* coronation rite, there is a sequence in which the king circumambulates the assembled brahmans, prostrates himself before them, removes the dust from their feet, and receives their blessing. (After the king's wedding, the *abhiṣeka* is repeated annually.)

After his daily morning ablutions, and before his worship of the five deities, the king sits on the throne, and after he washes his hands he bows down to the *rājaguru* who blesses him. Then the *rājaguru* performs the *maṅgalāropana* to the king; it is explicitly devoted to conferring auspiciousness (*maṅgala*) upon him. It consists of the *rājaguru* touching the king's forehead, while reciting *vedic* invocations, with objects placed on a tray, such as earth, lamp, fruit, grass, flowers, turmeric, mirror, curd, white mustard seeds, ghee, gold, raw rice, sandal paste, cloth, ornament etc.

Later in the same morning the king is led into the inner sanctum of the Jagannātha temple where he witnesses the bathing of the deities. The king bows to the deities, touches their jewelled lion throne with his forehead and circumambulates it, and sips some of the bath-water. He then goes to the *mukti maṇḍapa*, salutes the assembly of sitting learned brahmans by touching the ground with his forehead and receives their blessings.

Needless to say, the king cannot participate in the main offering to the deities which is offered in the inner sanctum behind closed doors by the appropriate brahmans entitled to conduct the *pūjā*. The gods do not eat the food of a king who has no *purohita* (says the *Aitareya Brāhmaṇa*).

In line with the orthodox *dharmashāstric* formulations, it is the king who wields the *daṇḍa*, the rod of punishment; but he is expected to rule in consultation with the assembly of learned brahmans, the *rājaguru*, the heads of monasteries (*mahanta*), *sannyāsi* (renouncers) and saintly persons. The *mukti maṇḍapa* of the *śāsan* brahmans can act as a court and can prescribe penances for offences committed by members over whom it has authority, but it is the king who inflicts the punishment of justice, even upon the said brahmans.

All in all, such evidence confirms the contention that in the Hindu context the Brahman is "superior" to king as *dharma* is to *artha*.

The Thai royal tonsure ceremony (*chūlakantamangala*)

One has only to compare the foregoing example from Orissa with the Thai royal tonsure ceremony performed in the mid-nineteenth and early twentieth centuries to appreciate the subordination of the court brahman vis-à-vis the king.[14]

Although the brahman officiant (*paahm*/*praahm*) enacted the chief ceremonial role in the topknot ceremony performed for commoners (he as the *purohita* cut the first lock of hair of the candidate and marked his or her forehead with the *unalom* sign and tied the *sincana* string round each wrist), in the royal ritual he has been "degraded." It is the king first, followed by the chief princes, who cut the hair and the chief of the wardrobe who shaved the head of the royal candidate. Again, although the lustral water was prepared by the brahman officiants, it was the king who poured it on the head of the prince of highest status (*chao fa*), and it was the king who received the tonsurate on Mount Kailāsa as Śiva and aspersed the prince. Finally, another sign of the brahman's degradation, was that he tied the *sincana* string on the ankles (and not the wrists) of the prince, wrote the *unalom* sign on his left palm (and not on his forehead), while it was the King and the senior princes who marked the forehead.

Concluding comments

How does the Buddhist patterning of ideas iluminate the Hindu conceptualisation of "purity" and "auspiciousness." At the cost of simplification,[15] it seems to me that the triangular relationship between renouncer, brahman, and king (who may be taken to encompass his subjects) are quite different in the classical Hindu (Indian) and classical Buddhist (Southeast Asian) contexts.

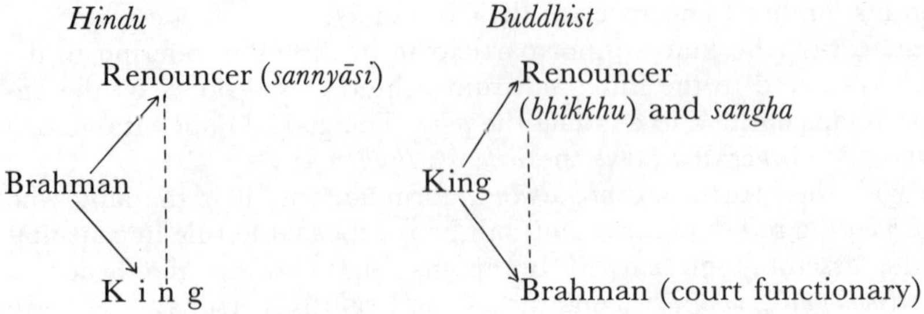

In the Hindu case Brahman and King are members of *varṇa* social orders, while the *sannyāsi* is either the peripatetic wanderer or later the member of a "sect." It might be said that the Hindu system's centre of gravity lies with the brahman who has a double relation to the renouncer whose ascetic values and "purity" associated with the transcendental quest have touched him, and to the King and to all householders in general to whom he represents Vedic and *dharmasāstric* learning and for whom he performs auspicious life-affirming rites, as the intermediary between the cosmic deities and the earthly overlords. The duty of these overlords is to sponsor the brahman's rituals as *yajamāna* ('sacrificer'). In the triangular relations, the direct relation between king and renouncer is somewhat weak (though by no means absent, as evidenced by the royal support for certain renouncing sects). Overall, the dominant pair is the brahman and king, and the brahman is "superior" to the king in moral valuation.

In the Buddhist case the point of articulation is the King, who as the foremost householder and regulator of society (*dharmarāja*) has a direct relation to the *bhikkhus* whom he must protect and materially support so that they may follow their higher path of purification freed from worldly entanglements and illusions. The brahman or his counterpart are ritual and scribal functionaries, who serve the king in the sense of performing all the rites and arts on his behalf to secure auspicious (*maṅgala*) well-being and prosperity for the kingdom at large. Thus in the Buddhist case the path of purification (*viśuddhimagga*) is radically separated from the pursuit of auspicious well-being, one assigned to the *bhikkhu* and the other to a brahman-type agent. Moreover the king and laity have quite separate relationships to these agents: to the *bhikkhu* they make donations in search of merit and in respect of his superior vocation, to the brahman type officiants they give rewards for services rendered. And in Buddhist "ideology" as presented in the "historical" chronicles composed by monks, it is the king's benefactions and support of the *sangha* that earns him praise and his legitimation. And kings have on account of such support of Buddhism assumed the title of *bodhisattva* (the future Buddha). The relation however between the officiant of life affirming rites and the *bhikkhu* have been weak or indirect. In the villages, typically young men served for brief periods as monks (or novices) and returned to lay life having acquired "merit" and maturity; and as elders they become eligible to perform *sukhwan* life affirming rites. At the royal courts the brahmans in due course became Buddhists and practised their trade under that affiliation, otherwise they were segregated from the *sangha* as such.

This comparison thus leads us back to the complex posture of the brahman in Hindu society. The "model" brahman of Hindu society simultaneously faces in two directions, and thereby "embodies" and practices or promotes both "purity" and "auspiciousness" as the Buddhists understand these values. He is a householder and performs auspicious rites; at the same time his position in society is integrally related to his "ascetic" regime exemplified by his attempts to control his sense doors, his fasts, his vegetarianism, his scholarly study of the Vedas, and his periodic retreat into meditation. This duality it would seem is the basis for complex statements about the quintessential brahman's purity and auspiciousness, and also how these values relate in Hinduism to life in the world and to *mokṣa* (salvation). Among humans, the brahman has the greatest component of the "pure" constituent of *sattva* in his material nature which entitles him to be of the highest *varṇa* status; he is also attracted to the purification of his senses that is associated with the renouncer's concept of *paraśuddha*. Correspondingly there is the auspiciousness (*śubha*) associated with the promotion of worldly interests, and with the processes of world formation and the divisions and partitions of orderly space and time; and there is the auspiciousness of final union and consummation with the cosmic deity, the attainment of *mokṣa*.

In any event there is evidence of a new brahman synthesis in the classical era, though scholars may not fully agree on the circumstances that led to it. Heesterman[16] focuses on the change in thought and ritual action in the classical era by which the brahman interiorised renunciatory values as an integral part of his identity. While not rejecting the view that renunciation emerged as a protest against brahmanical orthodoxy, he tries to show how renunciation was already implied in classical brahmanical ritual thought and became salient at the time of the new synthesis. Be that as it may, it is of great interest to us that the true brahman comes to be defined as "the renouncer or the interiorized sacrificer": he does not injure life, controls his senses, studies and teaches, sacrifices and officiates, is a *brahmacharin*, and for him the world is equal to his self. This renunciatory ideology "opens a way for the brahman to enter viable relations with the world without losing his purity," the secret of his ascendancy over life in the world being grounded in his "impartiality." A way has been found for fusing priesthood with renunciation.

Features illustrative of the double relation of the brahman to the world renouncer and the world affirming ruler are found in medieval mythology. Veena Das' exegesis of the caste *purāṇas* of Gujarat, such as the Dharmanya Purāṇa written sometime between the 14th and 15th centuries, treats the triangular relationship between brahman, *sannyāsa* and ruler.[17] For example, the myth of "The Creation of Dharmanya" says that six-thousand Brahmans learned in the Vedas were created from the mouth of each of the three gods who together meditated on the three Vedas. Moreover, the vocation of *sannyāsa*, defined as an ashrama lifecycle rite, is associated with the *varṇa* life-style of the brahman.[18]

The myth of "The Creation of Vanikas" enumerates the following as the activities of the Brahmans created by the three gods: some meditated, some performed *Yajña* (fire sacrifice), some performed *yoga*, some spent their time in acts of devotion to God, and others contemplated the ethics of political action (*rājniti*). Thus the brahmans had no time for household affairs, and the Vanikas were created to do household work for them.

In still another myth ("The Story of King Aama") the Brahmans claim to be ascetics and householders at the same time: "O King! *yatis* [ascetics] are those who are above happiness and sorrow and are not influenced by praise or insults. We [i.e. those who have been successful in controlling their senses] are the followers of the *grihastha-dharma* [dharma of householder] and are experts in the learning of Vedas and Vedangas..."[19]

It is quite likely that in the history of Brahmanical ideas and practices, it is the influence of early Buddhist and Jaina ethical values and practices, that transformed the moral and ritual horizons of the Vedic Brahmans, and made them relate their vocation to the renouncer as much as to kingship and the society in general.

I have earlier mentioned the explosive nature of the early Buddhist (and Jaina) polemics against the Brahman's advocacy of sacrifice, his adherence to materialistic and "bodily" notions of impurity-purity tied to caste and *varṇa* exclusiveness. The most corrosive influence of all might have been the inescapability of the processes of death and dissolution, and the need to confront it rather than to segregate it.

The brahman in due course seems to have incorporated as part of his code of conduct and religious regime some of the renouncer's aims and teachings, and thereby became "two-faced," one face looking towards the renouncer's ascetic code and borrowing from it the "pure" conduct of restraining the sense doors and abandoning animal sacrifice, the other face looking to the sphere of this-worldly action and officiating at auspicious and "pure" life-affirming rites. Significantly, within the ranks of the brahmans themselves, superiority comes to be accorded those who devote themselves to learning and who withdraw from priestly and temple functions.

NOTES

1 The three constituents of material nature (*guṇās* of *prakṛti*) are purity and transparency to consciousness (*sattva*), energy, passions and royal virtue (*rajas*) and heaviness, darkness and opacity to consciousness (*tamas*); these attributes are successively credited to the Brahmans, *Kṣatriyas* and the lower *varṇa* orders. These cosmologial categories appear in Sāmkhya Philosophy.

2 The Path of Purification (*Viśuddhimagga*) trans. Bhikkhu Ñānamoli (Colombo, 1956).

3 By Bhikkhu Ñānamoli in his introduction to the translation cited above.

4 Note, however, that certain portions, like the discussions of *sīla*, relate to the laity also.

5 *Dhūta* is glossed as ascetic; ascetic because he has shaken off defilement. *Anga* is glossed as practice.

6 I shall not in this essay deal with the implication of the fact that these "opposed" paths cannot be totally separated in Buddhism, for there are dynamic tensions that bring them into an interrelation. The figure of the *Bodhisattva* is an instance of the perfected saint postponing his liberation so as to work on behalf of mankind. The concept of *siddhi*, or supranormal powers, that become accessible during meditation, is another instance: although the renouncer is exhorted not to be tempted into using the powers in the world but to ascend higher into liberation, yet the *Viśuddhimagga* itself gives stories of the Buddha and his left-hand disciple Mahāmoggalana using their power of *siddhi* to perform astounding feats. Finally, in Sri Lanka, Burma and Thailand, the recitation by monks of *paritta* chants to give protection to laymen is a highly institutionalized expression of the monk's involvement in lay welfare.

7 For a reconstruction of the social organization of Northeast India, see R. Fick, *The Social Organization in Northeast India in Buddha's Time* (Calcutta, 1920). Fick says that the king in the "old" Buddhist era employed brahmans as *purohita* (advisers), astrologers, intermediaries in rites addressed to gods, etc.

8 According to Quartich H. A. Wales (*Siamese State Ceremonies*, London 1931) groups of Indian Saiva Brahmans reached the Thai peninsula between the 8th and 12th centuries A.D.; also Nakhorn Sri Thammarat recruited brahmans from these sources. After the destruction of the old capital of Ayudhya in A.D. 1767 by the Burmese, those who were able to do so escaped to Nakorn Sri Thammarat, whence they were recalled at the foundation of Bangkok (p. 19).

9 There were of course, outside the royal cosmic rites I have referred to, Buddhist festivals in which royalty and laity conduct merit-making rites at the monasteries. These festivals have to do with events in the career of the Buddha (e.g. *Visākha Būcha*: the day on which the Buddha was born, attained enlightenment, and passed away), or celebrate Kathin at the end of the *Vassa* (rainy season) when monks emerge from retreat, and other occasions associated with the history of Buddhism.

There is a rich documentation of court ritual, and the pattern of participation of brahmans and *bhikkhus*, for Thailand. Some sources are: Quartich H. G. Wales, *Siamese State Ceremonies*, op.cit.; K. E. Wells, *Thai Buddhism, its Tonsure Ceremony as performed in Siam* (Bangkok (1875), (1976); S. J. Tambiah, *World Conqueror and World Renouncer* (Cambridge Univ. Press, 1976); G. E. Gerini, *Chulakantamangala, the Tonsure Ceremony as performed in Siam* (Bangkok (1875), (1976).

10 G. H. Luce, *Old Burma—Early Pagan*, Vol. 1 (New York, 1969), pp. 69-71.

11 See A. M. Hocart, *Kings & Councillors* (Cairo, 1936).

12 See my *Buddhism and the Spirit Cults in North-east Thailand* (Cambridge University Press, 1970), for a detailed analysis of the roles of *bhikkhu* and *mau khwan* or *paahm*, and the relationship between these careers.

13 Frédérique Marglin, *Wives of the God King: The Rituals of Hindu Temple Courtesans* (Ph. D.

thesis Brandeis University, 1980; due to be published by Oxford University Press). An authoritative study on the historical and (some) contemporary features of the cult is A. Eschmann, H. Kulke, and G. C. Tripathi, *The Cult of Jagannath and the Regional Tradition of Orissa*, The South Asia Regional Research Programme of Heidelberg University (New Delhi: Manohar Publications, 1978).

14 G. E. Gerini *op.cit.* is our main source for this section. The main sequences of the royal tonsure ceremony were: (1) *paritta* chants by *bhikkhus* and their subsequent feasting (2) the cutting of the topknot (3) the aspersion of the candidate (4) the performance of the ceremonies of calling the *khwan* (*thamkhwan/somphot*) (5) the candle ceremony (*wian tien*) and (6) the throwing of the cut hair on the waters. As mentioned earlier, the *bhikkhu's* role is that of reciting the *paritta* chants at the beginning, and then that of receiving gifts (*dāna*) thereby conferring merit on the givers.

15 There are many categories/groups of brahmans as there are many types of renouncers with their specialisations; secondly there is a whole spectrum of kings from *cakravartin* or *rāja rāja* (king of kings) to lesser kings (*samanta*) and vassal chiefs. Yet general observations of the sort I am making are meaningful.

16 J. C. Heesterman, "Brahmin Ritual and Renouncer" in *Wiener Zeitschrift für die Kunde Süd- und Ostasiens*, Vol. 8. 1964, pp. 1-31.

17 Veena Das, *Structure and Cognition, Aspects of Hindu Caste and Ritual* (Delhi: Oxford University Press, 1977).

18 Das writes "The Dhaumya tells the story of how Dharmanya, the best place of pilgrimage, comparable to the Brahman who is the best of *varṇas* and *sannyāsa* which is the best of ashramas, was created" (p. 19).

19 *Ibid.*, p. 30.

Conclusion
Axes of Sacred Value in Hindu Society

JOHN B. CARMAN

Harvard University, Cambridge, U.S.A.

THERE ARE TWO WIDESPREAD PICTURES of Hindu society in the West. One is of the yogi performing great feats of physical and mental gymnastics, wandering through the world with his begging bowl or sitting motionless in the forest, deep in meditation. The other picture is of the Brahmin priest-scholar at the top of a vast hierarchy of hereditary communities that do not intermarry or even eat together outside the caste. The first picture is supported by the Indian philosophies elaborating various paths that renounce the world and lead to eternal salvation. The second picture has its scriptural support in a different set of sacred texts, the "law books" (*dharmaśāstras*). The first picture is summed up in the word for its goal: *moksha*, while the second is expressed in that Indian term with such a broad cluster of meanings: *dharma*.

It was the force of the first picture that led Albert Schweitzer to conclude that Indian civilization was not concerned with ethics. Both Schweitzer and his modern Hindu critics share the view that "ethics" is part of philosophy, and modern Hindu thinkers have therefore tried to demonstrate that Hindu philosophy does *not* have a negative view of the world and that its fundamental ethical principles provide a creative basis for Hindu moral action in the modern world. In classical Hindu thought, however, "ethics" was distinct from "philosophy;" i.e. *dharmaśāstra*, reflection on *dharma*, was in a different sphere from *darśana*, reflection on the path to *moksha*. Many treatments of *dharma* acknowledge *moksha* as the supreme goal of human life, but the pursuit of *moksha* is generally thought to require different practices and different attitudes than that of *dharma*, which is concerned with living in the midst of society, especially discharging the responsibility of raising a family and providing for its material needs. It is true that certain common virtues are acknowledged, especially the basic five of telling the truth, refraining from injuring living beings, remaining chaste, not stealing, and not being attached to possessions. Jains and Buddhists made a less stringent form of these precepts the basis of lay ethics, just as the more severe form is the moral basis for monastic life. Among Hindus, however, these common virtues are practically less important than the responsibility of each group in society to practice its *svadharma*, the specific lifestyle expressing its own particular nature. The action appropriate for particular groups at particular stages in life is what is taught in the treatises on *dharma*.

We have made considerable progress in understanding the ambivalent relation between *dharma* and *moksha*, but thus far we have not paid sufficient attention to the relation of both to two other legitimate goals of human life: *artha*, which means both power and wealth, and *kāma*, the satisfaction of desires. Both the traditional king and the married woman embody a value closely related to *artha* and *kāma*, the value of auspiciousness.

All the papers in this volume are concerned in various ways with understanding the nature and manifestations of auspiciousness, and most of them quite directly address the question with which our conference in Washington was concerned: the relation of the auspicious to another category that has received much more attention, both from social scientists and historians of religion: purity. Our assumption in organizing this discussion was that both purity and auspiciousness are values with fairly obvious expressions in Indian society, and that both, moreover, represent fundamental scales of value pervading Hindu social structure. Are both dimensions of some deeper single value, or must one or both be further subdivided into categories that better fit the realities of Indian life? Then there is the further question of whether, and in what respect, either purity or auspiciousness or both relate to the spheres of Hindu existence outside of family relations and political activities in society. In particular, are they also significant in the world of ascetics?

Directly and indirectly we have dealt with the problem of translation: have we chosen the most appropriate terms in English to convey Indian cultural realities? Are, indeed, these categories translatable? All the contributors are aware of this problem: the danger of imposing an external scale, or of bifurcating what is a single Indian category, or—conversely—of merging two distinct realities. The "caste system" is sufficiently different from social institutions in other societies that there is little danger that the Western observer or the modern interpreter in India is falsely imagining that there is some well-articulated Hindu social system, but the institution can easily be misinterpreted, either by failing to recognize how radically different caste hierarchy is from Western categories or by exaggerating the differences.

The word "auspicious" sounds a little strange and old-fashioned in modern English. Dr. Inden has commented on the derivation of the term auspicious from the Roman practice of augury, specifically by interpreting the omens provided by birds. No one else has discussed the range of meanings of the English terms, but Dr. Madan refers in a note to a statement by Jesuits in Delhi that "the word 'auspiciousness' has no standard use in their language other than in references to the 'superstitions' of pre-Christian European peoples and of non-Christians generally" (Page 25-26, Note 2). Dr. Madan does not say what "their language" is. Certainly in English the word "auspicious" is not so completely foreign; we do have some sense of auspicious occasions even if no augury has been performed! It is true, however, that auspiciousness is one of many terms "dug up" by Western students from the pre-Christian past of European cultures and used to describe religious phenomena in non-Western cultures. To some extent this is also true of the word "religion." Auspiciousness suggests more than simply good luck, yet neither traditional Christian orthodoxy nor post-Enlightenment rationalism has a meaningful category for this significant religious survival in folk and popular cultures.

"Purity," on the other hand, has a rich history of associations in Christian and Jewish traditions, yet it, too, is somewhat out of place in a modern rationalistic culture in which what is physically clean has no necessary spiritual significance and what is spiritually pure has no generally accepted content. Auspiciousness is not a "modern" Western concept. Purity to a limited extent still is, but both concepts retain sufficient meaning to help us to grasp the meaning of a number of related Indian terms, of which the two most important seem to be *śubha* and *śuddha.*

In Figure 1, I have tried to place the various aspects of auspiciousness and purity to which our attention has been called in the preceding papers. No one, it seems clear, has argued that the pure-impure axis is really the same as the auspicious-inauspicious axis. Considering the course of previous discussion that Dr. Marglin has sketched in the Introduction, this is quite remarkable. There have been diverse opinions on the significance of these concepts, including Dr. Inden's suggestion that purity be understood as *adhikāra*, qualification to perform a particular role. Dr. McKim Marriott, unfortunately *not* represented by a paper in this volume, criticized "purity" as a Western concept inappropriate to the "fluid" reality of Indian society.

The bottom half of the diagram refers to the this-worldly temporal realm, and it is here that Dr. Madan's contrast is most illuminating: *śubha* (auspicious) is an adjective primarily attached to the (opportune) time for performing significant acts, while "the notion of auspiciousness is also associated with places, objects and persons connected with the kind of events or actions mentioned above" (p. 13). The word *śuddha* (pure), on the other hand, "refers to the most desired condition of the human body or, more comprehensively, the most desired state of being. *Śuddha* and its opposite *aśuddha* are attributes of animate beings, inanimate objects and places with which a human being comes into contact. ...The notion of perfection in the sense of freedom from error or fault is extended to certain actions" (p. 17). Moreover, "degrees of *śuddha*-ness are recognized so that gold is considered...more *śuddha* than, say copper" (p. 17). The basic contrast, Dr. Madan concludes, is that "auspiciousness/inauspiciousness refers primarily to events—and ultimately to life itself as an event-structure" while "purity/impurity is basically an attribute of things" (p. 24).

Dr. Madan does not deal with the metaphysical or "otherworldly" significance of either *śubha* or *śuddha*, but it is not altogether clear whether the Kashmiri Brahmins he has studied do not themselves use these terms in such a philosophical way or whether such usage is to be considered metaphorical or figurative, as he suggests is the case with the reference to "auspicious married women" and "inauspicious widows" (p. 24-25).

The concept of *sattva* is crucial to the Brahmanical sense of superior purity. Dr. Marriott's presentation at the conference was the only one that questioned whether it was appropriate to relate the usages of *śuddha* with those of *sattva* in a single concept. In any case, *sattva*, the pure quality or strand in material nature (*prakṛti*) clearly belongs below the line in my diagram and is also clearly distinct

Figure 1

Relations between Purity and Auspiciousness in Indian Religion and Society

Auspiciousness out of Time or in Divine Nature	*Purity (śuddhi) relating to the path to release*
MOKSHA	
The Goddess Śrī	The ultimate goal conceived as totally different from life in the body
The auspicious qualities of Vishnu	
The beautiful Divine forms and adornments	Advaitic identity
The celestial company around the Divine throne	Yogic conquest of matter and motion
	Jain isolation (*kaivalya*) of the victorious self from the material body and world
Transcendent pure matter (*śuddhasattva*)	Buddhist *nirvāṇa*
Salvation conceived as a hierarchy of finite beings (from the demiurge to a blade of grass) all constituting the glory of Infinite being	Saiva union without distinction
The path to salvation as devotion to God in both the transitory and eternal realms	The path to the good conceived as complete purification (Buddhist *viśuddhimagga*) radical renunciation (*sanyāsa*)
Lay sanctity	
Divine descents to the temporal realm	*Paradoxical inversion of worldly values*
Auspiciousness in Time (śubham)	*Purity relating to Caste Status* *sattva* (the pure quality of matter)
DHARMA	
Interpretation of omens and astrology	
ARTHA and KĀMA	
The ruler and the realm	The cleansing of space
The brides of God (*devadāsīs*)	The protection of pure substance
Auspiciousness of women of all castes	The Brahmin and the lower castes

from that reality which transcends material nature altogether. This is the self/Self, which has purity (literally "stainlessness," *amalatva*) as one of its defining attributes. Among those groups that make less sharp the distinction between the spiritual and material realms, however, the special matter of the Divine forms is conceived as *śuddhasattva*, which might be understood as *sattva* separated from the other two *guṇas*, but is usually conceived as a special kind of matter that is substantial but totally distinct from any product of the three *guṇas*. I shall return later to a possible significance of the *guṇa* scheme as such for our inquiry.

Both Dr. Inden and Dr. Narayanan have dealt with conceptions of auspiciousness that concern both the temporal and the transtemporal spheres. Dr. Inden has explored the aspect of auspiciousness closest to the original Roman context of the English word, the interpretation of omens, which can also be seen as the human effort to discern all possible clues about worldly fortunes emanating from another and superior world. Beyond and beneath the realm of planetary deities is the Cosmic Person (Purusha). The Sanskrit name is the same as the designation of the pure spiritual reality over against all matter, but this view of Purusha is unitary and comprehensive rather than dualistic, thus all good fortune in this visible world has its source in the invisible body of the Cosmic Person. Dr. Narayanan has given examples of Śrī Vaishnava rituals illustrating both the this-worldly and transcendent dimensions of auspiciousness, but both are connected as manifestations of Auspiciousness personified in the Goddess Śrī (Lakshmī), Consort of Nārāyaṇa, understood as the Supreme Lord.

Dr. Marglin has emphasized in her earlier papers the importance of the category of the auspicious, the link between royal power and the special powers of women, and the sharp distinction between the axis of purity/impurity and the axis of the auspicious/inauspicious. Her essay in this volume discusses the relation between the positive and negative poles of each axis. Neither opposition is exclusive (privative): the pure and the impure are sharply separated when movement goes in one direction, but not necessarily so in the reverse direction, while the auspicious and the inauspicious in some circumstances can coexist, as they do in the contrasting moments of birth and death that both form part of the ongoing life process. It is striking that the ritual with which the article is particularly concerned is the installation of new divine images (Naba Kalebara) every twelve years. If it is correct that the axis concerned with the life process is more fluid than that concerned with the bounded substances, it should thus also be the case that the boundary line between matter and spirit, and between time and eternity is less definite in the sphere of auspiciousness than in the sphere of purity.

The papers by Dr. Jaini and Dr. Tambiah amply confirmed our initial hunch in planning this conference. For Jains and Theravāda Buddhists purity is confined to the spiritual realm and does not apply to certain material substances or to certain hereditary groups. Auspiciousness applies strictly speaking to the secondary "goals" of this-worldly life, though auspicious

Figure 2

A Model of Hindu Orders Of Value

Moksha contradicting *Dharma* and excluding *Artha* and *Kāma.*
Renunciation (*sannyāsa*) of society and pursuit of liberation (*moksha*).

Temporal Purity

Hierarchy of caste structure based on preponderance of pure matter (*sattva*) over passionate matter (*rajas*) and dull, heavy matter (*tamas*)

	Temporal Auspiciousness	
The Brahmin	"Good Luck" or well-being in the present temporal world symbolized in the	*Dharma*
higher than the king or the wealthy merchant	wedding (*maṅgala*), in married women whose husbands are living, in the king or prince	takes precedence over
All three higher than artisans and laborers	pursuit and enjoyment of wealth and power (*artha*)	*Artha* and
	satisfaction of physical desires (*kāma*)	*Kāma*

Each caste has its own specific duties (*svadharma*), fulfilling which helps one attain purer material bodies higher in the caste scale in future lives.

Seeking liberation in the midst of society through detachment from worldly goals.
Moksha including Dharma and transforming Artha and Kāma.

A contrasting Model of Buddhist Orders of Value

The true and noble dharma of the Buddha

Purity

Auspiciousness

The worldly dharma of king and householder

The Community (*sangha*) of monks and nuns

language is applied to victories in the spiritual realm. The two quadrants of otherworldly purity and this-worldly auspiciousness are therefore significant. This-worldly purity, on the other hand, is the heterodox sphere of Brahmin pretensions, and otherworldly auspiciousness is the realm of metaphorical language that links temporal fortune with the higher victories of the renunciant life. Dr. Hiltebeitel's paper explores some of the ways in which the two sets of opposition function in the Hindu Epics, stressing the reversal of roles between the two epics as well as the frequent transitions within each epic from the language of purity to that of auspiciousness.

The two diagrams in Figure 2 relate the axes of purity and auspiciousness to the four recognized goals of human life (*purushārthas*), known collectively as *caturvarga*. The form of the diagrams is influenced by the second and more abstract meaning of hierarchy in Louis Dumont's *Homo Hierarchicus*; that is, not with the internal arrangement of castes in the Hindu caste system, but with the relation between the pure/impure axis that Dumont considers basic to caste and certain other axes of values in Hindu society. These other axes are (1) that between the auspicious and the inauspicious and (2) that between the renunciant and the householder. If we use Professor Dumont's notion of the encompassing and the encompassed, it is possible to arrange these spheres in three concentric squares. This is in deliberate contrast to the diagram in Figure 1, in which no attempt is made to place auspiciousness and purity in hierarchical relation. The point of the second diagram, however, is not only to modify Dumont's scheme in certain respects but also to show that Dumont's notion of hierarchy itself contains the possibility of a reversal of values from a different perspective.

The innermost square is well-being in the present temporal world, called *saṃsāra*. This corresponds to the ancient Roman notion of the *saeculum*, but while it is of this world, it is not secular in the modern Western sense, for it is filled with powers that either aid worldly well-being or threaten it. For most Hindus the most significant ritual events take place in this sphere, and the central ritual is marriage, the auspicious rite (*maṅgala*). Economics and politics are in this sphere, both included in the single concept of *artha*, for the power to rule and the fruit of rule are so closely connected. Every householder tries to amass wealth; as long as he lives his wife is the concrete embodiment of auspiciousness, shown in her colorful saris, her makeup, the jewelry she wears, and most simply and directly in the red dot on her forehead.

The middle square represents the hierarchy of caste structure arranged according to the Brahmin's scale of values, in which the pure element of matter (*sattva*) ranks highest and may be considered a link to a higher purity that transcends material nature altogether. This is the sphere in which *dharma* takes precedence over *artha* and *kāma*, and in which *karma* may be accumulated to better one's lot on the same scale of *sattva-rajas-tamas* in the next existence. A person's purity on this scale is relatively fixed for the present lifetime, but it is possible to follow a more ritually pure (i.e. more Brahmanical) life style than is the norm for one's caste, and such relative purity of life will bring great karmic reward.

The outer square is concerned with purity in a more radical sense. Purity for one who has renounced life in society goes in principle beyond all the strands of material nature, even its purest strand, *sattva*. Such indeed is the theory behind the shocking reversal of worldly values dramatized by some early Hindu ascetics, who flaunted the laws of pollution by living in graveyards and using human skulls. In fact much Hindu asceticism in recent centuries has been less radical, making a more positive link with the purified life style of Brahmins and others. In the devotional movements, moreover, auspiciousness as well as purity has been concerned with a transcendent dimension that links in symbolism the well-being of the temporal world with the overflowing riches of God. In such thinking the category of *kāma* moves from the lowest human aspiration to the highest, a transformed desire no longer for a human partner but for the Divine Spouse, and a transformed attachment no longer to material things but to the Divine Lord.

If you compare the three Hindu squares with the two Buddhist squares suggested by Stanley Tambiah, you will see how much more complex is the Hindu value structure. The Brahmin is in the middle, looking Janus-faced in two directions: participating in the worldly goals of every Hindu householder but, at least in theory, preoccupied with a pure life style that will prepare him for the total purity of the transcendent realm.

The Buddhist king represents a significant value, but he defers to the Buddhist monks. The Hindu hierarchy may at first appear similar. The Hindu king is supposed to bow to the Brahmin and the Brahmin to defer to the ascetic. But in terms of their understanding of themselves and their world, many Brahmins have not deferred to the renouncers. They have claimed the all-encompassing category of *dharma* as their own special prerogative and have tried to limit ascetics to a small and well circumscribed share of social reality: a possibility at the very end of life for the very few who are spiritually qualified. There are, moreover, some hints of a time when Hindu princes did not acknowledge the superior status of Brahmins, and such occasional protests have continued from some groups apparently lower in the caste hierarchy.

These three distinct circles of value seem to me clearly present in the Hindu perception of social reality even though the ranking of the ends is less clear and may vary from group to group and especially from circumstance to circumstance. This multivalent perception may make it easier for the Hindu in the modern world to add another circle, the values of Western modernity, even when such values seem in conflict with traditional attitudes.

For participants in traditional Hindu society the questions raised in this collection of essays may not be significant. Abstract definition of principles and values may not concern those who incorporate such principles and values into the rhythm of their daily lives. The questions are significant, however, for those who stand outside traditional Hindu society but for various reasons want to understand it. This ''outside'' includes not only scholars in other parts of the world but also members of the various religious minorities in India. In varying degrees, moreover, modern educated Hindus view their traditional society from a new and external vantage point. For all such "outsiders" who are close enough to care about how and why traditional Hindu society functions as it does, the nature of the Hindu social system and the value structure of Hindu culture are matters of both curiosity and concern.

Sociologists and anthropologists may place their questions in a framework that applies theoretically to all societies and all forms of human culture, or they may want to concentrate on the categories specific and perhaps unique to Hindu society. In either case the present inquiry is affected by the history of scholarship concerned with Indian society.

Historians of religion concerned to relate "Hinduism" to the worldwide history of religion share many of the same interests as contemporary social scientists, but the question of the relation of purity and auspiciousness in India also has a particular background in twentieth century discussion in history and phenomenology of religion. The initial axiom of this field of study is surely that religion is a sphere of human life potentially present in all cultures. In previous centuries the constant elements in definitions of religion were generally beliefs in God or the gods and belief in the immortality of the soul.[1] Both the growing knowledge of religions missing these "essentials" (notably Buddhism) and the growing secularization of Western European culture led to some change in definition and certainly a shift in emphasis. Emile Durkheim's work had emphasized for sociologists the distinction of the sacred from the profane, but for historians of religion the new emphasis was especially signalled and defended in the successive editions of Rudolf Otto's book, *Das Heilige*, translated into English as *The Idea of the Holy*. A few years before its publication, however, Nathan Söderblom had written an entry on Holiness for the *Encyclopaedia of Religion and Ethics*, which he begins as follows:

> Holiness is the great word in religion; it is even more essential than the notion of God. Real religion may exist without a definite conception of divinity, but there is no real religion without a distinction between holy and profane....Not the mere existence of the divinity, but its *mana*, its power, its holiness, is what religion involves.[2]

Thus holiness (or sacrality) was not only a particular category in Western academic studies of religion but a super-category, defining as it did the nature of religion. This kind of emphasis has continued in much subsequent scholarship and has become particularly influential in American academic circles through the many writings of Mircea Eliade. Once such an emphasis is there it is important to determine the concept or concepts in each religion that correspond to the presumed universal category of holiness.

In India as in many other countries the religious historians' efforts at translation had been preceded by translations of the Bible into many Indian languages. In many such translations the term holy (*hagios*, *qaddosh*) is translated by a word meaning pure. In the Protestant translation in Telugu, the equivalent of Holy Spirit is *pariśuddhātmā*, the "completely pure Self" (the Roman Catholic translators did not agree, but they had no better alternative; they simply transliterated the Latin *Spiritus Sanctus*).

There have also been repeated translations of significant phrases from Indian languages into English. The same word *śrī* (auspicious) that is the favorite Sanskrit designation among Śrī Vaishnavas for the Goddess Lakshmī is regularly translated "Mr." when used as the honorific before a man's name, but before the name of a cultic center or an authoritative figure, *śrī* is usually translated as "holy" or "sacred". (The same multiple usage is true of the Tamil equivalent *tiru.*)

If "pure" and "auspicious" are synonymous or even closely related in Hindu usage and sensibility, no problem arises. When I began my studies of Hindu thought in India I assumed that this was the case. In my study of the God-concept of Rāmānuja I soon noticed that two types of phrases almost always occurred together in descriptions of the Divine nature. The first is "utterly opposed to anything defiling" (or alternatively, "without a trace of impurity"): the second is "ocean of auspicious qualities" or some similar phrase. I assumed that these were merely the negative and positive expressions of the same concept of holiness. In the light of the contributions to this volume I now have to ask whether many Western historians of religion, myself included, have been combining quite distinct Hindu values because both were considered equivalent to "holy". To some extent that may indeed be the case, but the situation is still more complicated. In his article Dr. Madan (p. 20) voices his regret that M. N. Srinivas "includes auspiciousness and purity in the encompassing category of the good-sacred." It is quite possible that Dr. Srinivas has been influenced by a Western concept of holiness. Initially, however, he brought out the great importance of auspiciousness for the Coorgs and treated auspiciousness as equal in importance to purity. This coordination of values at the social level might well have been reinforced by his Śrī Vaishnava tradition, in which all human values, among which purity and auspiciousness are preeminent, have their truest exemplification and deepest meaning in the Divine Nature. Many other Hindu traditions, not only those with Brahmanic leadership but also non-Brahmin movements in which householders exercise leadership, have also gone much further than Buddhist or Jain traditions in seeing a congruence between purity and auspiciousness, both at the mundane level and at the supramundane level.

Identifying the Western concept of holiness with either the Hindu concept of purity or the Hindu concept of auspiciousness would be a mistake, but the Western concept of holiness itself is complex, related to wholesomeness and health as well as to the "wholly other", to miraculous healings as well as to a "consuming fire", to the beauties of the bridal pair as well as their unblemished purity, and finally to a mystery of Divine simplicity that lies beyond the theologian's distinctions. We ought to be able to correct our mistakes and improve our "translations" while gratefully acknowledging the religious affinities that have helped us to gain such understanding as we have thus far achieved.

The concentration of this volume on auspiciousness and the emphasis on its distinction from purity is surely justified by the imbalance of previous scholarship. Much remains to be done, however, in analyzing the terms that can be translated with the English word "pure". It seems to me that they are sufficiently related in Hindu ritual and theological usage so that we may properly speak of a cluster of related concepts concerned with purity. The one that seems most significant for the caste hierarchy is the concept of *sattva* in the context of the view of material nature (*prakṛti*) as consisting of three qualities (*guṇas*). I await with interest the completion of Dr. Marriott's analysis in which the three *guṇas* are related to three categories of social process: marking, mixing and matching. I would suggest in the meantime that the triad of *guṇas* may be an early Hindu acknowledgement that social relations and human action may be more complex than can be indicated by any single axis of value. Each *guṇa* is distinctive and needs to be positively understood; neither *sattva* nor *rajas* is simply to be understood as the contrary of the other. *Tamas* would appear to be the opposite of both, i.e. both transparency to transmaterial consciousness (*sattva*) and goal-directed energy (*rajas*). *Tamas* is presented in such negative terms as to lead one to wonder whether those in society said to exemplify it might not have defined its distinctive quality rather differently. Certainly *tamas* seems to be that which gives matter some of its most obvious characteristics, notably its opaqueness and its heaviness.

The unifying thread in the foregoing papers is the lifting up of the notion of auspiciousness, a notion that is significant for both the state and the family and certainly relates to the values of bearing and rearing children as well as to the financial undergirding of the family. Our difficulty in achieving some academic understanding of auspiciousness may be in part that those who exemplify it most clearly—princes, married women, and *devadāsīs*—have not expounded it in a system of teaching, and it has been subordinated in the theoretical scheme developed by the intellectual spokesmen of the Hindu tradition, male Brahmin householders and ascetics. Yet there may be a further difficulty: we find it difficult to conceive of "good luck" as a meaningful category in ethics, whether Western or Hindu.

Eventually, however, we need to return to reconsider the categories that are apparently more familiar. Is there an overall concept of purity expressed in different usages? There are clearly different forms of impurity expressed by different terms. Is there a sufficiently general notion of impurity to justify our speaking about "forms of impurity"? Finally, there is the relation of both purity and auspiciousness to the concepts we thought we understood: *moksha* and *dharma*. We have already noted how Hindu sensibility connects both purity and auspiciousness in different ways to both *dharma* and *moksha*. *Dharma* itself is more than the observance of proper distinctions; it is the fulfillment of the distinctive capacity of each particular kind of being and perhaps the enhancement of being in general. The primordial Purusha, on which Dr. Inden has placed his reconstruction of classical Indian polity, is a symbol of a cosmic unity and a cosmic order that is dynamic rather than static, that involves sacrifice, but sacrifice for the sake of cosmic enhancement and well-being. The multitude of subtle distinctions have been important to the Hindu artist as well as to the Hindu scholar. Once our attention is called to such distinctions we can pursue them with great vigor. It is more difficult from the outside to get some sense of the whole, whether of Hindu society or of the cosmos perceived by that society, within which these distinctions are held, whether in repeated clashes or in a vast harmony. It is that sense of the whole that we need to pursue in the midst of our continuing investigation of the pure and the auspicious.*

NOTES

1 Cf. John B. Carman, "Religion as a Problem for Christian Theology" in *Christian Faith in a Religiously Plural World*, ed. Donald G. Dawe and John B. Carman, (Maryknoll, New York: Orbis Press, 1978) pp. 83-103.

2 Nathan Söderblom, "Holiness (General and Primitive)," in *Encyclopedia of Religion and Ethics*, ed. by James Hastings, Vol. VI (New York: Charles Scribner's Sons, 1937), p. 731.

*There are many points of similarity between the discussion in this volume and Dr. Veena Das's study, *Structure and Cognition, Aspects of Hindu Caste and Ritual* (Delhi: Oxford University Press, 1982). I am particularly struck with Dr. Das's diagram on p. 143 of the Epilogue based on the axes of purity and auspiciousness. I have benefited from discussion with Dr. Das but have been unable in this chapter to pursue her proposals with the care they deserve.

I have discussed many of these same subjects in a rather different form in an essay entitled "The Ehtics of the Auspicious: Western Encounter with Hindu Values," in *Foundations of Ethics*, ed. by Leroy S. Rouner, Boston University Studies in Philosophy and Religion, vol. 4 (Notre Dame, Indiana: University of Notre Dame Press, 1983), pp. 167-83.

CONTRIBUTORS

JOHN B. CARMAN, Parkman Professor of Divinity and Professor of Comparative Religion in the Harvard Divinity School, is the Director of Harvard's Center for the Study of World Religions. He is the author of *The Theology of Rāmānuja* (New Haven: Yale University Press, 1974), editor of the 1967 Consultation Report, *Study of Religion in Indian Universities*, co-author with the Rev. P. Y. Luke of *Village Christians and Hindu Culture* (Lutterworth Press, 1968), and translator of W. Brede Kristensen's lectures in phenomenology of religion, published under the title, *The Meaning of Religion* (The Hague: Martinus Nijhoff, 1960).

ALF HILTEBEITEL is Professor of Religion at George Washington University. Following publication of his *Ritual of Battle: Krishna in the Mahābhārata* (Ithaca: Cornell University Press, 1976), he has continued work on the Indian epics, with recent work focusing on the relation of the two epics, and on the South Indian cult of Draupadī. A study of the relation between the classical *Mahābhārata* and the *Mahābhārata* as it is represented in the Draupadī cult is now in preparation, based on fieldwork in India in 1975, 1977, and 1981-82.

RONALD INDEN, Associate Professor of South Asian History and South Asian Languages and Civilizations at the University of Chicago, has written *Marriage and Rank in Bengali Culture* (University of California Press, 1976) and *Kinship in Bengali Culture* (University of Chicago Press, 1977), with R. W. Nicholas. His current work focuses on the metaphysics and history of kingship in ancient and early medieval India.

PADMANABH S. JAINI has taught at Benares Hindu University; the School of Oriental and African Studies, University of London; the University of Michigan, Ann Arbor; and since 1972, has been Professor of Buddhist Studies at the University of California, Berkeley. His most recent works include *The Jaina Path of Purification* (Berkeley and Los Angeles: University of California Press, 1979) and a critical edition of the *Paññāsa Jātaka: A Collection of Extra-canonical Jātakas from Southeast Asia* (London: Pali Text Society, 1983).

T. N. MADAN, a social anthropologist, is a faculty member of the Institute of Economic Growth, Delhi. His research interests include cultural pluralism and social organization. He is the editor of the well-known journal, *Contributions to Indian Sociology*. His most recent publication is a festschrift in honor of Professor Louis Dumont entitled *Way of Life: King, Householder, Renouncer* (New Delhi: Vikas, 1982), of which he is the editor.

FRÉDÉRIQUE APFFEL MARGLIN is Assistant Professor of Sociology and Anthropology at Smith College. She is the author of *Wives of the God-King: The Rituals of the Devadāsīs of Puri* (Oxford University Press, 1985) as well as of several articles on Hindu rituals, myths, and images of the feminine. Her current research focuses on royal rituals in Orissa.

VASUDHA NARAYANAN has taught at DePaul University (Chicago) and is currently Visiting Assistant Professor in the department of Religion at the University of Florida (Gainesville). Her publications include several articles on South Indian Religion; she is the co-editor of *God of Flesh, God of Stone* (Anima Publications, 1983). She is currently working with John Carman on the translation of the *Tiruvāymoḷi* and its "Six Thousand" commentary.

STANLEY J. TAMBIAH is Professor of Anthropology at Harvard University and is author of *Buddhism and the Spirit Cults in Northeast Thailand* (Cambridge University Press, 1970) and *World Conqueror and World Renouncer* (Cambridge University Press, 1976). He has done field work in Sri Lanka and Thailand.

INDEX

INDEX OF AUTHORS

INDEX OF SUBJECTS